Praise 1vı ɪⲭɾⲁ////ⲭⲭ/⳼ⲭⲭⲭ//

"*Krantzman: A Memoir in Stories and Poems* combines humor and poignancy to present an author's life through poetry and prose, starting with profound coming-of-age themes and ending with the mires of addiction and finally redemption. Rob Cohen treats settings and characters as joyfully and abundantly as Saul Bellow, and readers will come to know 1950's and '60's Brooklyn as well as Augie March's 1930's Chicago. The poems are his own spare style but tenderly wrought in Modernist imagery like Ezra Pound's and H.D.'s work, an effective contrast with the prose. Cohen's unfortunate passing has been greatly honored. There's much to learn from his life and memory, told so lovingly here."
                Mike Freeman, author of *Drifting: Two Weeks on the Hudson*

"In this multi-genre text, reminiscent of Michael Ondaatje's work, Rob Cohen captures the sights, sounds, and smells of his childhood in Brooklyn. He takes his readers on a sensory walk to Max's candy store during a time when it was perfectly fine to tie his dog outside the shop. At home, he shares his exuberance for the moment when he'd unwound the tin strip of the can and the aroma of coffee unleashed, and the scent of the cedar closet his grandfather built. The sounds of the foghorns and the music he loved waft through this book. Krantzman emerges and candidly shares the ordeals and fatigue of addiction, along with philosophical considerations of justice and fairness. The breathtaking opening lines of "Phineas Phipps," Krantzman's alter ego, make one only wish he could have written more. Nevertheless, Cohen's intellect and insight shine through this brilliant work."
            Jane M. Gangi, PhD, author of several books, including *Contemporary*
                Children's and Young Adult Literature: Cambodia to Darfur

"I've dreamed of this book. The dream of Cohen's lucid, unpredictable, and hilarious writing has come true, collected here, fully manifest. Very few writers can embody their imagination within so much tenderness and dark abandon. See a firecracker explode out of a grate above a white convertible, or "a bright blue flame erupting over the edge of the pan," or see him remember "the terms of surrender and slide out / the other side / clean" and you will experience how Cohen operated with empathy rare to find, even at his most ironic. I owe my own writing life to his inspiration. I am grateful to have each of these pieces as open, replenishing oases. "
                Dan Kraines, author of *Licht* and *Makhtesh Ramon*,
                            and Rob's former student

KRANTZMAN

A MEMOIR IN STORIES AND POEMS

ROB COHEN

Riddle Brook Publishing LLC
Peterborough NH

Cataloging-in-Publication Data

Names: Cohen, Rob, author. | Reilly, Mary Ann, writer of introduction.
Title: Krantzman : a memoir in stories and poems / Rob Cohen ;
introduction by Mary Ann Reilly.
Description: Peterborough, NH : Riddle Brook Publishing, 2024.
Identifiers: LCCN 2023945135 (print) |
            ISBN 979-8-9859413-4-0 (paperback) |
            ISBN 979-8-9859413-5-7 (ebook)
Subjects: LCSH: Alcoholics--Biography. | Addicts--Biography. |
            Brooklyn (New York, N.Y.)--Biography. |
            Boston (Ma.)--Biography. | Twentieth century--Biography. |
            Autobiography. | BISAC: Heading / Subheading. | BIOGRAPHY
            & AUTOBIOGRAPHY / Personal Memoirs. | FAMILY &
            RELATIONSHIPS / General.
Classification: LCC HV5032.C64 A3 2024 (print) |
            LCC HV5032.C64 (ebook) | DDC 362.292092--dc23.

This collection includes fiction. Any reference to any persons, living or dead, is
purely coincidental except in the case of historical persons.

Library of Congress Control Number: 2023945135

ISBN: 979-8-9859413-4-0 (Paper); 979-8-9859413-5-7 (EPUB)

Cover art © 2022 by Mary Ann Reilly
Cover design by Orphee
Copy Editors: Renee Charney, Gabriel Vanore

Riddle Brook Publishing, LLC
Peterborough, NH
www.riddlebrookpublishing.com

for those still suffering
& for those
who refuse to change

CONTENTS

The sun goes down
The stars come out
The room gets dark
The dreams come out

—bathtub song, 2002

INTRODUCTION

Introduction

Mary Ann Reilly

ANNE LAMOTT OPENS HER writing memoir *Bird by Bird* by saying, ". . . good writing is about telling the truth. We are a species that needs and wants to understand who we are." This quote resonates when I think about the poems and stories selected for this book. They are ruthlessly honest, and I would be lying if I didn't also say that rereading them here has been difficult for me, as so much of the young man I first met those many years ago is revealed.

I fell in love with the author of this book thirty-five years ago when we met in graduate school. During that first day, in a writing course, we were asked to talk about a book that influenced us as writers. The usual collection of works surfaced, from Dante to Steinbeck to Dickinson. What caught my ear was Rob mentioning an American writer, Richard Powers, and the intricate and woven retelling Rob gave of Powers' *Three Farmers on Their Way to a Dance*. I had neither read the book nor knew of Powers, but Rob's description had me finding a paperback version of the novel in a bookstore. I read it within a week.

Across the next three decades, I would come to know the man, through marriage, parenting, and caring for him through his too-early death. Throughout his lifetime, the man I met at school six years clean and sober would remain so. These stories and poems chronicle his youth, his addiction and alcoholism, the various city neighborhoods he lived and worked in, and his absolution. What they don't tell you is what came after: how he dissolved the family vending business (originally begun by his grandfather on West 36th Street in Manhattan) for a new career, both creating and recreating himself at the same time. I was a high school teacher then, and Rob told me with some marvel that he'd never met anyone who loved what they did for work as much as me. So Rob, in his late thirties, became an English teacher in New Jersey—work he too honored.

I want to close this introduction with a story about Rob that says as much about him as any. Years ago, Rob immersed himself in the writings of John McPhee, spending the better part of two years reading book after book, including a series about the geological history of North America (later collected as *Annals of the Former World*, which I have now as an e-book). So it wasn't surprising one early spring afternoon when Rob asked if I wanted to hear McPhee, who was giving a talk at Princeton University where he has taught nonfiction writing since 1974.

The night of the lecture, we left home and traveled to Princeton. It must have been in the mid-1990s. I can't tell you what McPhee said, only the excitement I felt at coming up against lofty ideas and then discussing these with Rob as soon as we left the auditorium and all through the nearly two-hour drive home. This is what life with Rob was so often about. He was all energy and thoughts and passion and questions. At the time I was a doctoral student at Columbia University where I had gone to learn how to write theory. These discussions with Rob fueled many of the ideas I would later work with when it came time to write my dissertation.

A decade later Rob, our ten-year-old daughter Emily, and I got in the car and headed west on holiday. We had no destination in mind. This is how we most often traveled. Just get in the car and drive somewhere. On this trip I was most often photographing something, while Emily was lost in Harry Potter. Meanwhile, Rob was again experimenting with sound, a new and admittedly fascinating obsession. On this trip he had strapped an audio recorder to the front of the car with the idea of making sound collages. Rob insisted that I read (and he reread), at the very least, the second book from the *Annals* before setting out, and so we did. This volume—*In Suspect Terrain*—chronicles the geological history of New Jersey. After reading parts of the book, I knew driving through western New Jersey would never be the same. McPhee—and Rob—helped me to see landscape differently.

We wandered west, then south, then west and north until we got to the Badlands in South Dakota where our too-old car broke down.

This is what life with Rob was most often like.

Part adventure. Part meditation.

This combination of adventure and meditation frames the stories in this book.

Editor's Note: Rob Cohen had a number of writing influences, including early twentieth century modernists and the later post-modernists. In his writing, Cohen has adapted a number of conventions taken from these styles, including single (open) parentheses, squeezed words (in which two words are shown together without a space between), and various invented portmanteaus. These appear in the text as he intended, and should not be considered typographical or printing errors.

Neighborhood Stories

Dogs and Bagels

On Sunday mornings my parents would sleep in. I'd learned not to wake them early because it was never very pleasant; instead I had this little transistor radio my father had won at some convention or other, or maybe that he'd gotten as a promotion in the mail. (Later there'd be an even smaller one that belonged to my grandparents, but that was a good one and I couldn't have it—I also don't think they ever finished marveling at the technology of miniaturization.)

I'd sit in my room in the early pre-dawn and put my radio on very low, so that I could barely hear it, and listen to the *WMCA Good Guys* on AM 570, one of the earliest of what would later be called Top-40 radio, a station that was always in competition for the number-one rating with WABC and Cousin Brucie. But I always liked the *Good Guys* and wanted nothing more out of life than a *WMCA Good Guys* sweatshirt with it's silly oval face drawn with roughened edges to make it look like it had a beatnik's beard and hair.

I wasn't allowed to make myself breakfast because I'd either make a mess or too much noise or both; the dog would be asleep in my parent's room and I'd just lie on my bed with the door closed and that terribly harsh overhead light on, listening to the songs of the time (Dawn / Go away / I'm no good for you, by the Four Seasons, or We'll have / Fun fun fun / 'Til your daddy / Takes your T-Bird away, by the Beach Boys, or any one of a half-dozen different Beatles songs that were on the charts in the early part of 1964), until the high reverb fast-talk of the DJ became a blur of sound that lulled me back to sleep.

When I'd wake again it would be light and I'd dress myself, get ready to take the dog for a walk. But it was Sunday and there was nothing so simple as that. My job was to get the bagels (sometimes I'd forget to put the garlic ones in a separate bag and catch hell later when my parents got up and "they all tasted like garlic") and the newspapers and my reward: a comic book. (*Fantastic Four* or *The Avengers* usually. I wasn't much on the DC superheroes, though I sometimes got *The Brave and the Bold* which always had two or three heroes in one story.) I'm thinking now that my father gave me maybe a dollar for all of the above, and there would still be change I was allowed to keep for later.

I'd take the dog around to the avenue where the bagel store was and tie him to the meter, run into the shop and get a dozen bagels (for three people), a big bulky warm bag on a too-warm-for-that-early-summer morning and then walk on around to the candy store.

Walking down Avenue Z I'd pass the house where Rocky lived: Rocky was a Siberian Husky who stood taller than me when he reared up on his hind legs, and barked at everyone else but for some reason loved me. I could put my fingers through the cyclone fence and he would lick them; if I put my face up to the fence he'd lick my face and he never even bothered about my dog, a little long-haired frankfurter dog, a dachshund uncreatively named Schnapps. So I'd say good morning to Rocky. (There was another Rocky that lived on the block years later, a black dog that barked at everyone and even made me feel afraid from time to time—me, the kid who could pet your attack dog without asking permission and get the dog to lick my hand; I'm thinking here of a Belgian Shepherd who became my best friend in a brickyard one time). After the Siberian (the first Rocky) would be the bus stop along the corner house with the very low wrought iron fence and then across 28th further along Z, past Christie's where I'd get my hair cut, the Chinese laundry where it always smelled of steam and starch and where you could see Mrs. Chinese Laundry always ironing in the back. Her husband the proprietor, the one who'd interact with the customers, had an abrupt speech it took me a long time to learn to understand. I know now it was a thick Chinese accent and with that memory a flood of faces come roaring up to meet me. David Wong for class president of PS 98 when Sonny Liston fought Cassius Clay. *Csillagánc*, a Hungarian dance we had to learn in second grade and which I dubbed Chili-garbage and was not allowed to participate in, all my classmates envious— Russell, who lived on my block, Richie Stier, Neil From, Douglas Weiss, Thomas Drugas. Or third grade when a kid named William who seemed a little slow got caught playing with the beads that were permanently attached to the top of his desk, right next to the inkwell, beads that were supposed to be used to teach us counting, the red ones are ones, the green ones are tens or something like that, and Mrs. Rothstein yelling *William, meet the beads, beads, meet William* in her shaming class, later, me in tears because I didn't read a book, a girl name Ivy getting a fourth grade teacher by the name of Pearl L Gross onto a kid's TV show called *Wonderama* as a teacher of the week. Or seeing two kids on the corner fight, Wong and somebody—Was he the launderer's kid? Did they live upstairs? And Dougie saying that Christie kept a naked girl playing the guitar in the back of his barber shop and the day Christie showed us all how to use a top, spin it on his hand. Or the morning he won $140,000 in the Irish Sweepstakes.

But on the corner, opposite the public school that was to be mine through 4th grade until it was condemned—a story in itself, seems we didn't have a real principal, we'd had an acting principal, some putz

14

named Weitz. Something had happened that one of the mothers wasn't too happy about so she went up to the board in downtown Brooklyn to complain and the man behind the desk there said *where does your child go to school* and she said *PS 98* and the man said *Lady, that school's been closed for years,* and she said *then why does my child go there every day?* This when I was in the 2nd grade. By the time I finished 4th grade they had built a wing onto PS 52 a few blocks away and we were all transferred there. A bigger place with better facilities, and a vice-principal who only wore red socks—Mr. Savits, another putz.

But on that corner, across from PS 98, was Max's candy store. He ran the place with his wife and daughter, and knew all the kids by name; my job was to get the Sunday *News,* the Sunday *Mirror* (a Brooklyn paper), and pick a comic book. Schnapps would wait outside for me, tied to a different meter: I think now about the innocence of that time—no one would take my dog and a kid could walk around the neighborhood early in the morning and not have anything to worry about. So with two Sunday papers, a bag of bagels, and the new *Fantastic Four* in one hand and the dog's leash in the other, we'd wander home.

No one would be awake yet when I got back and I'd just put everything on the table and either read my comic or watch *Wonderama* or *Magilla Gorilla* on one of the local stations until my mother woke up and made breakfast. Or if I got too hungry, I'd wake her, peeling back an eyelid and asking: *Are you awake?*

Coffee Can

WHEN I WAS A SMALL CHILD, my mother would buy coffee in a tin can from the local supermarket, and it was always a treat when it was time to open a new can; I would break the special "key" from its nesting place on the bottom of the can and with minimal help thread it onto a special metal strip at the edge of the lid's outer rim, then unwind the strip of metal onto the key that separated the top of the can from the rest; when I was really small I would need help as the process went on and on and the thickness of the metal winding onto the key increased. But it was that initial hissing air rushing into the vacuum-sealed coffee can that I enjoyed, the aroma of freshly ground coffee escaping from where it had been trapped.

Rose & Villy

I HAVE TO TELL YOU ABOUT Rose & Villy—I can't stand it anymore, the story's just too good.

They were an older immigrant couple that lived across the street from us in our Brooklyn neighborhood, not directly across—that's where Izzy and his perfect garden were—but one over to the right as you faced the rowhouses on their side of the street. Rose & Villy lived upstairs with their daughter Judy, and rented their garage to us since they didn't have a car and we had two: my grandfather's and my father's. I remember going up there with my mother to pay the rent once and Rose gave me a box of chocolates for no reason I could tell. I also remember watching my mother hand her the rent; I think it was maybe five dollars but I can't swear to it, which even for then was probably pretty cheap. (This had to be 1958, maybe 1959. Either way I know I had only recently started regular school where we were expected to learn to read—which I basically already knew how to do—and to practice a perfect penmanship that I never mastered.) We had a peculiar green-colored Opel with a stick shift. And running lights between the doors on the outside, like a plane or a boat.

Herbie Klein lived next door then with his wife Judy (yes, I know, there are two Judys in this story, or stories, Rose and Villy's daughter Judy and this one, Herbie's wife, but the latter is incidental so you won't hear about her again), daughter Debbie, and son—Ricky? Ronnie? Ronnie. Ronnie had a chronic bed-wetting problem. Upstairs next door were Avis & Gene, and their daughter Bettina; and across the street where Izzy & Anna lived later on was another couple whose names I can't remember, but I remember the mother's red hair and that they had two daughters, Carrie & Donna. I remember hearing how the parents had gotten divorced later on. And then Izzy & Anna moved in and rented the downstairs apartment to Herbie & Rozzie who had a three-year-old son who had some kind of motor impairment and who the neighborhood took under its wing.

Back to my story: the one I started out to tell you.

There was a young man living downstairs from Rose & Villy who once gave me a football he caught at a pro game. Probably a Giants game. Nice guy. I'll be damned if I can remember his name but I can still see his crew-cut head as he reached into the trunk of his car and handed me that ball. I was as happy as happy gets. When I think of it now, it was a ball much like the footballs in old films, more round than the ball used now, with a bubble on one of the points. Maybe it was just a discard because of that bubble and it wasn't really from a Giants game, or maybe it was, but anyway I was thrilled with it and I'm sure he enjoyed making the neighbor's kid smile.

That still wasn't the story about Rose & Villy I'm trying to tell. But it's coming. Just one more last side trip, I promise.

My mother once observed that Villy (his real name was Willy, but he pronounced the *W* as a *V* and, as you'll see, there is a reason for the contemptuous imitation of his pronunciation I learned from my mother—in fact, I have difficulty thinking of him as Willy and not Villy because I never heard anyone say it any other way) was the kind of guy who, when he finished using the hose to water the garden, he'd take the hose and put it back where it came from: not like most of us who wind it on one of those handy hose hangers that mount to the wall just above the hose spigot. Not Villy. He put the hose *away*. Drained of any leftover water, it went back into the box it came in, with all the original cardboard spacers, and neatly arranged, the box closed so that it looked pretty much like it did when he first bought it at the hardware store. I was nineteen years old when I left that neighborhood for the last time and, so far as I know, Villy was still using the same box to keep his hose fresh and clean.

So maybe he was a little bit of a bug. Or maybe he was a lot of a bug.

Judy (Rose and Villy's Judy) was "sent away" when she lost it which, I think, was more than once. Why did she lose it? you ask. Well, I will tell you two stories (not just the one I planned to tell you, and maybe not even that one at all; I'm not sure yet). One is hearsay. But I believe it. The hearsay story is that Rose & Villy would eat steak for dinner and the kid would get an egg. Rose & Villy would eat what was normal for adults to eat, but the child didn't deserve anything good because she wasn't good enough. I imagine there were other far greater abuses that took place in that house, but in that innocent time no one took much notice—something along the lines of how unfortunate the child was, how crazy the parents were, all in whispers across porches, along telephone wires: we didn't even know families did this stuff except in movies and art, and as kids in that time in that neighborhood, we didn't know a whole hell of a lot about either—we weren't allowed to. So Judy was just never around, a kind of non-entity.

Let's move ahead to a time when all the guys on the block are a bit older and outside playing stickball (this, it turns out, is the story I've been wanting to tell all along, which is also, it seems the second story about how Judy lost it): it's after daylight saving time and school must still be in session because I'm not away for the summer. The neighborhood has changed a bit: Mickey & Dore live next door; Izzy owns the house across the street; Russell from down the block has become one of the guys. And so we have a game going—can't remember everyone who was there, but I do remember it was Mickey & Dore, me, Allen, Russell, and at least one someone else to even the sides. The important thing is that we're playing a schoolyard game, yelling and screaming, someone winning, someone losing, someone taunting, and across the street Judy's voice erupts from Rose & Villy's house:

"YOU TWO SHITS! HOW DARE YOU TREAT ME LIKE THIS! GET ME SOME STRAWBERRY ICE CREAM!"

Seems Judy had come home from the hospital (from one of the times she lost it, I guess) and her parents were at it again. Don't know what happened; don't even know when Judy got home. Could've been weeks but I doubt it. But there is her voice crashing across the early summer air. It's warm out but not so warm that everyone is sealed inside with the air conditioning. Instead, everyone has all the windows wide open which means they can hear everything and now parents begin to pour out of their homes. We've stopped playing, stunned. I think, more at the publication of the word *shit* than anything else.

"NOW, GODDAMMIT! YOU SHITS! YOU GO OUT AND GET ME SOME STRAWBERRY ICE CREAM!"

Mickey turns to me, maybe to all of us; we'd drifted from our positions on the street over to a group standing together, all on the verge of laughter, and Mickey says, just loud enough for us to hear: "What happened? She doesn't like chocolate?" and that was enough to put us over the top. We couldn't stop laughing, and on she went:

"YOU SHITS! I WANT STRAWBERRY ICE CREAM! GET ME SOME STRAWBERRY ICE CREAM!"

By now it's getting scary and even we know something is wrong, so we just all head home. Besides, it was getting dark anyway. Judy was taken back to the institution some time that night.

It wouldn't be home and it wouldn't be my family if that was the end of the story. So next night, we were barbecuing on the hibachi on our little porch upstairs and I was outside helping my father bring in whatever it was we were eating that night, hamburgers maybe, and probably corn on the cob, and as we were going in the house with a tray full of dinner, Villy comes walking up the block looking a little worse for wear. I duck into the house to hold the door for my father who has the tray in one hand, the barbecue fork in the other and, as he steps into the house he turns his head over his shoulder and hollers out, perhaps loud enough for Villy to hear: "Did you bring the ice cream, schmuck?"

Explosions

NOTHING BURNS UNDERWATER. We knew that because we had all seen water put out a fire at one time or another. That's why, when Allen said he had an M-80 he was going to light off and throw down the sewer, Russell and I began to laugh. Why waste a perfectly good M-80 on something as ridiculous as throwing it down the sewer where the water would put it out? Of course, the more we laughed, the more Allen and Dore became determined to prove to me and Russell that M-80s were treated with a special chemical that would let them burn underwater.

Dore got a match from somewhere, lit the fuse, and dropped the explosive through the grate on the corner diagonally across from where Russell and I were standing. As the minutes went by and nothing, absolutely nothing, happened, Allen and Dore became less and less sure that anything could burn underwater.

Allen would run up to the corner, carefully lean out over the curb, take a quick glance down the sewer to see if he could see the spark of the burning fuse, and just in case the M-80 was really going to go off, he would tip back over the sidewalk and run headlong down the avenue to the middle of the block as fast as he could.

(It may be useful to pause here for a more complete description of the intersection at hand. The north/south street was a side street—in fact, the one on which the four of us lived—and, as a side street, it was a one-way street, one-way south. The east/west cross street was a two-way avenue. This meant that the traffic which traveled along the avenue had the right-of-way. It also meant that each side street had a stop sign at the appropriate corner. Since this particular side street was a one-way south, the stop sign was at the northwest corner, the same corner where two young boys had tossed an M-80 down the sewer.)

Next it would be Dore's turn to test the water, so to speak. After a brief argument with his partner as to whether such an effort was at all necessary, Dore would hesitantly creep forward and repeat the same procedure: run/lean/glance/sprint. After the two alternated through several rotations, Russel and I began to heckle. With each shout we became more confident in our mutual conviction, and it began to appear as if

Allen and Dore would have to believe us. However, our friends on the corner opposite were holding on to the last bits of a rapidly diminishing faith.

About this time a large white convertible with its top down pulled up at the stop sign. The driver was one of those hard looking and somewhat overweight bleached blondes who worked the morning shift at the local diner and called all her regulars "honey" so as not to confuse their names. She had just had her hair done up into a beehive, a style aptly named and appropriately chosen.

Several feet to her right, next to the stop sign, bereft of any hope that a given army surplus explosive device would actually explode, unaware of either car or driver, Dore leaned out over the curb and stared fearlessly down in the sewer scanning for any sign of fire, any sign at all, while the blonde, oblivious, watched the traffic on the avenue and waited for her opportunity to drive on.

The water propelled up through the grate and over the stop sign before any of us realized we had heard the smothered *foomph* of the M-80 going off, then continued its parabolic journey to a point about thirty feet above the sidewalk, equidistant from both Dore and the blonde, where, subsumed by the greater force of gravity, it described a graceful downward arc which consequently caused a brief but filthy downpour in the general vicinity of the blonde sitting, until just that moment, oblivious in her, until just that moment, white convertible. Dore, already doubly stunned by the blast and his own simultaneous dousing, looked up to find an irate woman with a deflated hairdo getting out of her car and screaming something to the effect of, "I'll get you, you bastards!" Russell and I were consumed by laughter; although we had now realized there really *was* a chemical that could make a thing burn underwater, it didn't matter one whit that we had been wrong. After all, we weren't the ones drenched in sewer water.

As the blonde emerged from the now two-tone car, Allen and Dore whipped around and took off as fast as they could, due west along the avenue. She might have caught them if it weren't for the extra seventy or so pounds she carried. What a frightful sight to see a woman of her size and shape, dressed in white stretch pants and a white pullover stained with sewer water, gaining momentum as she lumbered after my friends.

Russell and I didn't stick around either. Even though we had nothing to do with anything—except for maybe some inciting remarks before the explosion—we, too, were small children easily frightened by the blonde's transformation into the beast now charging like an angry rhinoceros toward Allen and Dore. So I (and Russell, I assumed) ran home as fast as I could: up the front steps to the porch, through the front door and up the steps again to the landing, a left, up the last three steps, right to the kitchen, left to the dining room, and right again through the hall and past the bathroom to my room, safe.

◆ ◆ ◆

Our garage (the one that came with our apartment and not the one across the street we rented from Rose and Villy) was under the front porch and reached by means of a sloping driveway, a slope which produced a mildly torturous scraping sound against the tailpipe of the various cars my family owned over the years. The garage itself was a blocked-off corner of the basement, its back wall the flip side of the basement wall against which stood a cedar closet built by my grandfather for storage. That closet ran the length of the wall and was divided into two parts, each part divided into a smaller upper section and a larger lower section, with plenty of room for me, a stereotypically small child, to play in, while still tall enough to hang the big rectangular plastic storage bags which held winter wardrobes in summer and summer wardrobes in winter. I remember finding seven pairs of roller skates among the boxes on the slatted floor, boxes filled not only with skates and old toys but with grandmother things and old people things I didn't understand. Built into one side of the closet were the basement's only light bulbs, turned on by pulling a string which hung down just above my extended reach, requiring a small jump for me to grasp and tug, and which, when not readily found, initiated a mild anxiety that would escalate toward genuine panic, especially if I was in the basement alone, such as when my mother would send me down to get something, a journey wracked with apprehension and fear if I needed to search in the other side of the closet, the right side, the side I never went in because it was where darkness lived, floating endlessly in its perpetually colorless world.

Sometimes I would lie on my bed, tucked into the rear upstairs corner of the house, and let my mind wander out through the open window and along the ordered sprawl of streets and avenues we called *the neighborhood*: mirror-image rows of identical houses attached along common walls, an architectural monotony relieved only by the clustered shops and decaying projects: out past alleys and fences, past garbage trucks and vandals, whistlers and singers, lovers, dog walkers, muffled shouts and sirens, each mystery rhythmically merging into signals of evening departures, deliberate fishing boat foghorns reminiscent of ocean night sounds, a thousand stars pursued across the bay by a moonlit breeze as waves, explosions, crashed their way back to me and a place where I could sleep.

In my dream I would open the sliding door on the closet's left and there would be no fear, the light would already be on, and the smells of cedar mixed with my grandmother's fur coat, the residue of camphor and wool commingled with cardboard and dust, and even the skates and other toys would all together issue an enveloping aroma of warmth and love and joy. I would step into the closet and pass through its rear cinder block wall into a room both finite and boundless, dimly lit by bare bulbs hanging from the darkness above, full of huge stuffed animals alive and gifted with speech. Then the colorless man in the gaudy plain shirt erodes boundary and substance with speech that burdens the meaningless, dissipates scents as he comes ever closer and the glowing bulbs disappear one by one behind, time fades in the flaring light and I find myself awake, opposite my open closet door, a door closed every night for fear of things behind it.

◆ ◆ ◆

As I got older, the sounds changed. Foghorns and fantasies—once the source of dreams—now were nothing more than distraction: noise to keep me aware, restless. I had seen the boats and the people on them; I had smelled the dead-fish smell of peddlers and catch, watched scales in commerce and exchange: dollars from local restaurants, fresh seafood, catch of the day on hand-lettered menus—the discovery of the poor scrabbling over what couldn't sell honestly.

And I had new neighbors. The wife was an obese, pockmarked, loudmouth broad whose hair resembled a platinum polyester fright wig, and the husband was a fatter, loudermouther drunk who came home late most nights only to find she had already locked him out (I never could figure what he did with his keys until I got older and discovered for myself that one could reach a state where knowledge—say, the whereabouts of one's keys— and the ability to take them out of a given pocket and unlock a given door were mutually exclusive conditions.) He would try to break in and she would try to break him. They had no children of their own, but they did take in a stray.

Since their house was located at the back of the empty lot which lined up with my bedroom, I had a ringside ear for the main event each night. She would say *you sonnuvabitch, y'wouldn hid a man s'hard as y'hid me* and he would reply *you're right* and I could hear the fist embed itself in her flesh.

◆ ◆ ◆

I must have been sixteen years old when I was standing in the closet in my room having it out with my mother: it wasn't her demand I clean up my room, or even just that I clean out my closet, which irked me, but that somehow, in some vague and untouchable manner, I felt threatened. I was an adolescent who had been taught from the beginning of my education that I could be all and anything I wanted because all I had to do was go and get it. But somehow I couldn't, I lacked permission. I had begun to perceive a contradiction between what I had been told I could have and what I knew I could have, and the gap between the two was growing. I wanted peace. And now, in my closet, that order had come crashing down for what was to be the last time; my private fantasy, my escape hatch, had already been taken from me in favor of some larger purpose not apparent and unexplained: there arose in me a fascination with the notions of justice and fairness, of principle and action, and the discrepancies inherent in them when placed into operation. It wasn't until some six years hence when I was summoned to jury duty that I became acutely aware of the true basis for my animosity toward the world, that my search for peace and serenity was founded in true bloodless revolution, and that such peace was not available to me, not because I was to be found lacking certain necessary qualities or because I had failed to grasp a certain concept or faith, but because that peace was not inherent in my nature. In short, I made my own great leap forward and have remained suspended in mid-air every since.

Dumpster

So there's Ronnie and his kid Anthony standing on a pile of garbage: really. I'm not kidding about this; let me explain: Ronnie is a long-time customer but he's not what I'd call the most ethical or the most . . . what's the word here? . . . well . . . he's a scrounge; he'll use a used anything before he breaks down and buys a new anything: use it, refurbish it, sell it to someone, buy it back four years later when it's run down again, refurbish it again, and so on.

Ronnie was grown now, of course, but at one time was the kid who came into his father's business and had already been there for a few years when I did the same thing and became the third generation in ours;

both businesses involved with those machines that sat for years next to, say, the supermarket entrance doors so that the first thing any mother had to deal with the second she walked in was a kid whining that he wanted—no, *needed*—a nickle or a dime or whatever for a gumball or maybe a plastic egg with a cheap decoder ring barely visible inside. We sold the machines and the stuff that went in them to the Ronnie's of the world (or of New York City, anyway), while they (the Ronnie's of the world) leased the machines to the stores and filled them up, collecting the coins as part of what we called *the route*, a small percentage of said coinage then going back to the supermarket or corner store that housed the machines day to day.

With Ronnie I could never figure out all the angles: whether it was his father or his father-in-law who was the original owner and then he came in along with his brother? Brother-in-law? I don't know which body went with which marriage; all I knew was every somebody in the family touched the business some way, and they always paid cash and always bought a lot of parts because they were always fixing up used stuff, not just maintaining what they already had. And since they were old-line vendors originally from the Bronx, they had some of the oldest machines out there. I mean, one-cent bubble gum vending machines that were older than me, and so far as I know, they've still got as many of them out there as they can find parts for: that's what makes this so interesting. Not what I've told you, but what I'm going to tell you. About Ronnie. And Anthony who is his kid and who makes the third generation of their family in the bulk vending business.

See, when the time came for us to move out of the old building on 36th Street after forty-one years at the same address, the time also came to get rid of forty-one years of accumulated stuff. I'm not talking about old candy, although we did find some of that up on the second floor. I'm talking here not only about stands and machines and parts that hadn't been used for over thirty years. I'm talking about things that could no longer be used at all because the industry and, I suppose, the world had changed too much.

Up on the third floor, for example, there were some parts and boxes from a project my grandfather had completed by the time I was about six or seven years old. Plastic "atomic" rocket bubble gumball banks for kids. I understand that he and my father sold a ton of them. But that was in the late fifties and early sixties when the space race was just getting underway and every kid wanted atomic fireball candies and anything that said *atomic* sold twice as well as anything that didn't.

There was a seemingly endless number of things that went into that category (too old to be of use and why have we been holding on to it so long anyway?) so I called the garbage company and arranged to have them drop off a thirty-yard dumpster figuring that we probably, maybe, had enough of that stuff to fill one. We almost filled three. We found things to throw away that we didn't even know we had. I was tearing through all the parts, trying to figure out what we might want to keep (just in case) and what was actually obsolete when I came across a carton that had never been opened and which had no markings—they must have faded over the years. And I thought to myself: What bonanza might we have here?

In the old days packing was done a bit differently and each part was wrapped in newspaper. So, not knowing what I had in front of me, I opened some of the wrapping and found coin wheels (a small part in a coin mechanism on which the coin rides as the customer turns the handle) from a machine that had ceased manufacture in 1959. This was 1993. I was curious then, so I looked for the date of the page of newspaper I held in my hand; before I could see the date, I was struck by the headline: US MISSILE SCIENTISTS SHAKEN BY SPUTNIK. That puts it in '57? '58? Something like that. And this was the stuff I was throwing away. It was useless. (I would have kept the newspaper but it crumbled as I tried to refold it.)

Useless, that is, until Ronnie and Anthony caught wind of what we were doing. They had come in for some supplies and Ronnie asked a bunch of questions about what we were throwing away. And I told him that it was old crap that had been lying around for centuries, stuff we didn't need, stuff nobody could use. Did I mind if he took a look? Well . . . no.

About an hour and a half later I went outside to get some air (we'd been stirring up a lot of dust during the clean up) and there was Ronnie separating the contents of an entire, almost full, thirty-yard dumpster. He was going through what we had thrown out like a five-year-old given the keys to FAO Schwartz and told he could have anything he wanted so long as he could carry it away himself. And Anthony, who I always thought was more level-headed than his father—someone I'm sure would never even consider throwing an M-80 into the sewer—kept holding things up and saying, "What about this, dad? And what about this?" The pile of what was now theirs was becoming larger than the pile to be carted away. It was remarkable to me: they were taking parts for stands that not only couldn't be assembled, but for which the missing components hadn't been manufactured in at least twenty-five *years*; they were taking specially manufactured hardware that had no further purpose in life. We had some weights from an old scale but not the scale. They took those. Some globes for some old machines, but not the machines. They took those, too. They took anything that looked like it might have been brass at one time or another (there wasn't nearly as much as they thought). They took pieces of old machines that were not only beyond repair, but for which the parts probably didn't exist any more even if the machines could have been fixed. They filled their van and said they'd be back in a day or two for more.

Meanwhile, we had uncovered an old safe that maybe my grandfather had used before he retired in 1967 and which had the combination on the door and a few unimportant documents inside. This we managed to *sell* to Ronnie, but not before he made sure I understood that no one, absolutely no one, was to know that he bought a safe and that he and Anthony were going to have to figure out a way to get into the basement without any of the neighbors seeing. I didn't know his neighbors, and I didn't know what he was going to keep in there, but I began to think it wasn't just the bags of coins from his collections on his route.

There's one more thing I want to tell you about Ronnie: his belt. He had this black leather belt that he wore with his key ring clipped to it and the belt was as worn as any I've ever seen: we used to kid him about it. It looked as if it was about to wear through in several places at the same time, but he wouldn't replace it. Anthony even bought his father a new one for Christmas one year, but Ronnie wouldn't put it on, said the one he was wearing still worked fine and, besides, it was just getting broken in.

Getting to Know You

WE WERE AT WORK ON A HOT afternoon, a Friday in late summer, not exactly a busy time, what with all the kids away at camp or at the beach or on vacation: the heat of the city just seems to slow things down. And Mel, who runs the parking lot on the small bit of property that he rents from us (barely more than a double-sized driveway, really, just next to where we had our Manhattan-based candy-and-vending-machine business, said driveway then widening out a bit behind our building so that you could squeeze in maybe half a dozen cars) and I were getting a bit punchy.

Before I go any further with that story, I need to fill in a few details. We had two customers: Danny and

Ben. (We had more than two customers, of course, but just two customers for the purpose of this story.) Ben was once partners with his brother, Danny's father, thus Ben is Danny's uncle. After Danny's father died, he took over for his father and became partners with his Uncle Ben, but the two of them didn't really get along as business partners so they divided up the route, collecting the coins from their agreed-upon machines, then went their separate ways. However, this is not to say that they didn't get along as family—it's just that they couldn't be in business together. And sometimes they'd come into our place together because then they would have two vans to fill up with merchandise; what didn't fit in one would fit in the other. As long as they didn't have to work together on a permanent basis, they were fine.

Now every time they came to buy merchandise from us, they'd see Mel out there doing whatever he did in taking care of his parking lot: moving cars around, standing out in the street waving cars in, whatever. And, as a parking attendant it seems rather obvious that one would not refer to Mel as a fashion plate: he wore that green uniform that every parking attendant in New York wears and carried around all the keys to all the cars in a little cigar box. Like I said, the lot was very small and as a result he didn't want to build one of those shacks that you see around; he couldn't really afford to lose even one parking space.

Most of the time, in bad weather, he'd either sit in his car or come in and sit at one of the workbenches in the back of our place. And in the summer we were air conditioned so he'd be hanging around inside all the time. Not that we minded: he liked to kid around and we usually managed to have a few laughs during the course of the day.

Danny and Ben seemed to have a knack for catching Mel at something less than his best. In winter he always wore what looked like used clothes and the inherent prejudices against the kind of guy who would choose to be a parking attendant were enough to allow my father and me to convince both Danny and Ben— but especially Danny—that Mel was a couple of bricks short of a load. Missing a piece. Not playing with a full deck. However you might want to say it. It didn't matter that it wasn't true, Mel's behavior was erratic enough that it took very little to persuade anyone, really, that Mel was somehow the equivalent of, say, something Ronnie might salvage from a dumpster. It's just that *anyone*, in this case, always seemed to be Danny and Ben.

Once Mel got wind of what we had been telling these guys, he decided to play it up as best he could, (though I suppose it really didn't take much of an effort on his part, at that). Anytime either Danny or Ben would come in, Mel would do or say something strange enough for them to think there really was something wrong with him. And none of us, Mel included, did anything to disabuse them of the notion.

So it's a lazy summer Friday afternoon. And the Lincoln Tunnel traffic is doing the slow build to a standstill that makes the Friday commute such a joy for so many. And since we're not that far from the tunnel entrance, that means anyone heading our way at about that time is going to share that joy. So along comes Danny. Five minutes later, Ben. They've been alternately driving and sitting in traffic in their respective un-air-conditioned vans, and when they step into our warehouse/showroom (if you could call it that) with the air conditioning blasting frigid air, they relax a bit. After we've loaded their purchases into the vans (all of us working up a sweat in the heat), they come back in for a cold soda (we always kept a supply in the fridge in the back) and to shoot the breeze for a while: they've made their last stop for the day (us) and just want to kill some time and cool off before they begin the long haul home.

On this particular day, Mel had found a block of styrofoam about the size of a new cake of brown soap. He had taken that block of styrofoam and impaled it on a threaded rod about twenty inches long (the rod was a standard part from one of the vending machines we sold) and pretended it was a microphone. He would stand by the counter, sway from side to side, and sing *Getting to Know You* into his "microphone." The problem was he didn't know all the words, and Mel singing the first two lines over and over and over was proving too much for all of us. I wound up calling everyone I knew until someone could at least give us one entire verse, but because Mel couldn't read my handwriting after I'd managed to get the rest of the lyrics (thanks to my inability, as previously mentioned, to master the required elementary school penmanship lessons), I wound up singing with him at least once (though it might have been more).

But while Danny and Ben were sipping their sodas, and while Mel had slipped back out to shuffle cars for an exiting customer, Danny asked me why Mel was walking around with "that thing."

"You mean the styrofoam block on the rod?" I asked.

"Yeah, that."

And Ben, "Yeah, what's he doing with that?"

"Uhh . . . you explain it," I said to my father

"That's his microphone," my father told them.

Danny mouthed the word *microphone* without making any sound and began to laugh, then made some kind of remark about Mel being damaged goods. Of course, with that, Mel comes wandering back in, with his microphone, and when Ben asks him what he's got there, Mel nonchalantly explains that it's his magic microphone, that it helps him sing. Then Mel asked me to sing with him (which I politely declined). Shrugging, he put his cigar box full of keys down on the counter, positioned himself in front of one of the display racks where we could all see him, began swaying gently from side to side as if to get into the rhythm, and began to sing:

Getting to know you
Getting to know all about you
Getting to like you
Getting to hope you like me . . .

Godot, Again

TWO GUYS ON THE CATWALK of the George Washington Bridge, one holding a can of gray paint, and the other holding a brush . . .

POEMS,
SOME OF THEM LONG

Hell's Kitchen

I used to go out on Friday nights
& make sure I was 1st
to the bar
knock down a quick 6 or 7
& hide the evidence

a clean ashtray, no rings
on the tablecloth, no stirrers
lying around
when someone shows up
& asks
        if I've been there long

a few hours later
they'd all go home
& I'd head for the   next place
       and the   next
       and the   next
except once
when somebody said

    why don't we all go dancing

& I said
    I'll meet you there
    I'm gonna drive around
    & air out
       my head

I remember starting the car
on that cool summer night
cracking open the sunroof
cranking up the radio
& easing back on the clutch

& I remember an ambulance
the nurse telling me
I'd been in an accident
the hospital
the guy in the next bed
with a gunshot wound
a doctor saying

my body was so relaxed
it absorbed the impact

I had bruised
                all my ribs
& my breathing was labored
& my parents
took me in
gave me their bed
where I dozed until morning
light
showed me the mirror
still neatly centered
above my mother's dresser
opposite

I got up
with the intent of just
walking past
(I'd been avoiding mirrors for years
                afraid
of what I'd find
when I turned my head
at the last second

I looked just like
the guy with the long hair
& scrungy beard
who lectured his insanity

to an oak tree
every morning
when I'd lived in Boston
slept in the Public Garden
& tried to forget
all the things
I had made myself
into
acting the way my father had taught me
every Friday night
through high school
when we'd sit down
after he'd worked all week
& knock back a few

my throat began to close
with the hardache
that comes
just before the tears
begin to burn
& my eyes began to fill
with an image of myself
as I stood
in the center of my grandmother's living room
between 2 huge mirrors
hung on opposite walls
                    bent forward

my head turned
to the infinite
repeated image of me
receding
to a vanishing point

she'd called me
into the kitchen
where I couldn't see over the stove
it was all apart
the pieces were all around
& I wanted to see
what was up there
so my grandmother picked me up
& I reached for the pilot light
the bright blue steady blue flame
set my finger on fire
& she did nothing
nothing
to stop me

I ran upstairs
& pressed myself
into the corner of my parent's bedroom
between the shelves
& my father's valet
where I took down a book
read the 1st 2 words
got stuck
          at the 3rd

& brought it to the kitchen

my mother
from sink to counter to table
someone on the phone
was just too busy
to see me
against the refrigerator
waiting
to learn   how to say
              how to know
Ishmael

> *He's the one talking, telling*
> *the story,* she said. It's a man's
> name...*WHAT ARE YOU READING—YOU*
> *SHOULDN'T BE READING THAT*

& grabbed the book away
as if it were a glass shard
picked from the garbage
told the phone she'd call right back
dragged me
back to the books
& shoved into my still confused hand
a memorized copy of *The Cat in the Hat*
& left me there
until I was old enough
to go to work

Special Olympics

Geraghty
had already lost
both
        legs to diabetes
spent his days
supine
        although
(rumor had it
he did own crutches

Ralph
had to wear oversized
        overshoes

so he could walk
the streets
(his alcoholic neuritis
made him
The Enemy of the Ants

& the guy who lived across the street
with the *gornisht helfn* feet
moved so slowly
everyone knew
      he never
brought home ice cream
in the summer

so when Franklin #2
who thought
a microcassette taperecorder
was a reasonable substitute
for a walkman
said

    Why don't we stand
    the 3 of them up
    at the corner of 10th avenue
    give them each a push
    down 36th
    & see who wins

I thought 1st
of those little toys
with balanced legs
wobbling from side to side
as a weight
          suspended
over a table's edge
draws them forward
& said

          no—
          Geraghty has no legs

then wondered
if old starvin' marvin
could leave his
wine guzzling & windshield washing
franchise
at the far end
of the Lincoln Tunnel exit
long enough
to call the finish line
& finally asked Franklin #2:

          Do you think
          that if we could get them started
          they'd stop
          before they wound up
          in the middle of the tunnel traffic

or
do you think
        their momentum
                could carry them
                        all the way out
                                past 9th?

4:17 EDT, July 20, 1969

He was just
an old friend
danced on treetops
& lakes
so a kid
could believe in magic
when news came
theyd taken out a pole
with a piece of
colored cloth attached
stuck it
in his eye

Robert Cohen

and with one small step
maninthemoon
was dead.

Eagle had landed
in peace
clawed out moon's tongue
took it home
& said
dreams are made
out of rocks.

Soap Opera

The neighborhood wiz
fixed my tv
turned
on the set
& left
the sound off

musical conjures of
recordings
heard 1000x before
blare
in the foreground
as the picture sharpens

instrument and voice
slow
the pace of patterned colors
sound & image
coalesce
in sensory assault

on the screen:

actors
bereft of language
pose
as cameras dolly
pan & zoom
past
a family
dressed to kill
an afternoon
in a visual vacuum:
pop,
drunk as a cliche
in a 3pc persona
sculpted
from an empty silver flask

embraces mom,
baubled
      bangled
           & beaded

a dispirited character
who mouths
her performance
from a shopworn script
stored
       in a small vial

They cocktail.
They talk.

The bright hope of posterity
aged
       beyond her youthful character
daughter (20
portrayed by actress (30
       enters:
a 60s contrast
to conspicuous consumption
& its ostentatious display
made up
to appear without make up.

       (assume
       the phone has rung
       before
       mom picks it up

cut to:

the daughter's man
(husband, lover
a male
of a similar indeterminate age
looks a tough
macho crotcho with a
gingerbread face—
like some VALS packaged
male
left over from a GM tv ad
a few football seasons
ago

the daughter
        waves the mother off
as if to say
she's not there
but mom
(as mother's will
simply says
something
(we can see her lips are moving

cut to:

the man child
whose mock-anger is so poorly played
he looks
like an unbalanced
murderer
after masturbating
on his sister's drawers
in a locked closet

the phones hang up
on their respective cameras

the daughter
expresses dismay

      & I imagine
      tv music
      as the signal fades

      click
      flick

      around the dial
      & back again
      an incantation to
      catch
      a commercial

a woman, the character
of a housewife
dressed
in jeans
    & workshirt
(the agency has deleted
the bandana
since last I looked in

she
walks through the hall
answers
    the door

(this
    could be a house
    esp
    if you live in one
or
    could be an apt
    esp
    if you live in one
is
    what we might call
    the broadbased
    appeal

but who
was knocking at her door?

(come to think of it
she looks
conspicuously like a daughter
we met
only moments before

opens the door
to a gargantuan
toilet bowl
which
          having obviously planned
makes
its attack
chases
          the woman
all through her dwelling

(is it a house
or is it an apt
only the agency knows for sure

tv man says
this
is insane

& I wonder
     which
the ad
for supposing
that a giant toilet bowl
could make a point
when other means might fail

the show
for attempting
to make
     the same point
because
other means have failed

or the viewer
(me
for letting them in
for cementing permanently
these images
in the catacombs
of mind

     just what are they selling me here?

Hey—all you

Hey—

all you upwardly mobile
briefcase totin'
yuppietype individuals

how 'bout a little help for ol'
starvin marvin
onna corner here

Kafka

I was on my way back from the bank
walking along 9th avenue
around 39th street
when a man
wearing an undersized fedora
& a wrinkled polyester shirt
buttoned at the neck
accosted me

> *Pliz sehr, pliz*
> *I am Rosh'n man*
> *call to*
> *lawyer Tverski?*

he held up a slip
of paper
with the name TWERSKI
neatly drawn in uppercase letters
followed by the 7 digits of a telephone #

then handed me a quarter
& pointed to the piece of paper
as if it were an invocation
authority
to interrupt my afternoon

there was a pay phone
a few steps away
& I sensed this foreign man
was afraid
            & perhaps alone
in a very strange place

maybe he had been trying
to stop people for the past hour
& I was the 1st who would listen

or maybe he was just nuts
& this is what he does
on a summer afternoon in New York

(the context of the city
is always so hard to read

so I dialed the #
& waited through a series of clicks
& pauses
only to be reconnected
to a dial tone

I pressed the coin return
unsure of how to tell a man
who speaks
the few words of English
he's learned
since last Thursday
that this # wasn't right

my new ally
sputtered & flapped
until he said

>   *Forst, vun, syev'n ayt*
>   *in de Bwooklin*

which after a moment
I took to mean
dial 1-718 1st
because the # was in Brooklyn

this time I got a secretary
at a law office
& had to explain
I was calling for a Russian man
who knows no English
& who needs to speak
with a lawyer named Twerski
(who
       I was praying
       knew Russian

the secretary asked me my name
& I told her
it didn't matter

this man had stopped me
on the street
& I was at a pay phone

she told me Twerski was in court
he'd be back at 3, call then
& hung up

we stood on that windy corner
for another 20 minutes
2 men
with no spoken language in common
& struggled
to find enough humanity
to get the message across

my mind raced through what little
high school Spanish
I could remember
as if that would give me the words
I needed
while we gestured & pointed
drew pictures in the air
& said

     no
     nyet nyet nyet

over & over & over
until we were reasonably certain
we each had been understood

he couldn't call back at 3
he had to be somewhere else at 2
some other kind of court
or hearing

so I left him at that phone booth
to wander the maze of bureaucracy
that was his destiny then

On a Slow
Afternoon in July

dinners with the crew
newsmakers of 1959
a tour of the factory
models at a trade show

these pictures
chronicle my grandfather's career

I had taken them down
to store
on the 3rd floor
& as I carried them upstairs
tucked under my arm

I saw him as he was
4 years ago
when I walked through the doors
of the CCU
only to have the nurse ask me
to please
      help control him

(the night before
he had disconnected himself
from everything

I put the pictures down
to unlock the door
& when I saw his face
I remembered—
that trip to the hospital
was the first time
I had been back to Florida
in the years
since that Friday
my father called to me
up this same stairwell

     there's someone in the office
     I think you should know

when a man you've never met
says he's your grandfather's 1/2brother
& the moment runs like a cold drink

taken too fast after a sweat
how do you
answer?

this 1/2man with large ears
offered a story
of yet another brother
I had never known

somewhere in the Depression
my grandfather had a different business
& a partner
who swiped 30grand
& this brother

> can you lend me $2000 to get started
> again
>
> you don't need a loan, you
> need a job—come work for me

& my grandfather
walked

◆ ◆ ◆

on that slow afternoon in July
full of a passion for words
& drink
served downtown
at McSorley's Old Ale House
replete
        with eons of dust
& a city's history
Max told me
he'd never been on an airplane
I took a quick glance through the paper
found an ad for Miami $99 each way
& booked us
on a midnight flight
to God's waiting room

then left the bar
to go puke on a stranger's door

after I cleaned myself up
Max gave me his key
& told me to go sleep it off
        at his place
he'd pick me up there

I came to on a park bench
just outside Gracie Mansion
sometime after dark
with the key still in my hand
& raced out to Brooklyn

just in time
to be startled awake
by Max
ransacking his own dresser

on the plane
I gave him the window seat
flopped down with my legs in the aisle
& just stared
along the length of the empty cabin

a few drinks later
I noticed Max had lost interest
in the night sky
& was bent over
with the top of his head
pressed against the back of the seat
in front of him

he was making a kind of low gurgling
          noise
as he rummaged
through the open bag
on the floor
& I thought
he was going to be airsick
so I tried to distract myself
until he rapped me on the shoulder
with the back of his hand
& I turned

to see him thrust
his muzzy face
right through
the split seat
of the jeans he had grabbed
on the way out

the stewardess was so impressed
she bought the next round

back on the ground
Max & I were the only ones on the bus
when the driver asked us
why we didn't have any luggage
& I held up my knapsack full of papers
while Max displayed
his dirty red & white nylon ditty bag
& told the guy

just get us to the nearest bar

we strolled up route 95
draining last call from plastic cups
& I felt like a bad cliché
from a late-night movie
stuck
on some desolate predawn highway
with no hope for rescue
& no plans for the future

by 7am my clothes
were too heavy
a day old
& I was starting to sweat

we found a place to buy some shorts
looked down a side street
& took turns
trying to block the view
of passersby
as we changed
in a phone booth

all we needed now was a laundromat
& some sleep

so we rented one of those old but clean
airconditioned efficiencies
2 beds with a private bath
& by the time I woke up
Max had come back with beer
a pint of Irish
& some munchies

◆ ◆ ◆

I spent that night
in a bar full of hookers
& transvestites
lusting after the organist

with the band
        a big blonde
with long straight hair
standing in front of a confederate flag
& opening each set
with a flute solo
(Barnum & Bailey's bigtop circus
        theme

Max sat at the bar
next to a darkhaired woman
with a used up WolfmanJack voice
& wearing little enough
to show her tattoo-covered body
he ordered a beer & left
me with a barmaid
who only wanted to take me home
when her shift was over
if I could explain
'why I had left New York

so I told her
how I could still hear my father's voice
echo up the stairwell
& through the open door
the morning before
but she didn't get it

right after last call
one of the girls I'd watched

go in & out
all night long
offered me her phone#
& told me to call
in the afternoon
it'd be worth my while
& one last transvestite
dressed like the Blue Fairy
walked up to me
& said simply

wanna fuck?

& when I didn't answer
sashayed
        out the open door
to the stretch at the curb
& got in

I had $8

the flight back was full
of aggressive children
& that uneasy sweat
that comes only
when the booze has stopped
for a little too long
& the guilt tries to tell you
you've gone a little too far
again

Max and I hadn't said much all day
so we just split up
in the subway
I got home
to find my girlfriend
dressed
& ready to leave

I had forgotten
we were due
at dinner
with my family

she was supposed to meet my
       grandparents
up
from Florida
for a visit

◆ ◆ ◆

I was just standing there
on that 3rd floor landing
shaking my head
when I opened the door

dim light from opaqued windows
slanted across
piles of dried out cartons
left over

from projects and partnerships
my grandfather had abandoned
years ago
I left the pictures
on the floor
& reached inside the door jamb
for the lightswitch

fluorescent fixtures flickered
illuminating the green metal shelves opposite
& an old carton
of toys & games
I had left on the floor

I stood with the box in front of me
& tried to remember
what I had put in there
& when
I ripped it open
the 1st thing I grabbed
was my etch-a-sketch

I made a few tentative lines
across the years
then drifted back to the door
where I bent down to pick up
the pictures
& saw his face again

◆ ◆ ◆

my grandfather
my father
& I
sat on the terrace
overlooking everything
& kept the peace
with a bottle of scotch

& while the women hustled dinner
to the table
      we moved
inside
overlooking the terrace

it didn't take long
for conversation
to break down

my grandfather
raised an empty
salt shaker
held it out to my mother
& scolded her name
over & over
until she rose to fill it

my father turned to my girlfriend
& began
      that laughing alliance
which always cast me

as the butt of the joke
& made enough noise
to distract my mother
drifting
between table & kitchen
bringing & taking
too much

I sat opposite my grandmother
watching her chew
in that way she has
of forgetting
to close her mouth
while she scowls
at every morsel on her plate

my grandfather salted his
undressed salad
& as I passed him a roll
I threw him a curve

I didn't know you have a brother

maybe it was the scotch
or maybe it was the weekend
or maybe I'd just had enough
but whatever it was
it stopped him too

at first he just nodded
slowly
as if to say   oh   yeah
as if it were some matteroffact thing
I'd somehow forgotten
but then he got stuck
staring through his salad
at something he never let anyone see

I thought about who my greatuncle
might have been
        how much he might resemble
this man who sat next to me

did he also
explode without provocation
slam doors
against his wife's tears
& disappear
in a blind rage
only to gather that night
with his cronies
& their women
in a drunken card playing
freeforall
& spend the next day
hosting his wife's family
at some grandiose barbecue
where all the food was burnt?

my grandfather looked up
from his plate
& began to speak
in the gravelly voice
of an old man betrayed
by his own remorse

he spoke first about business
how he once had a little shop
on Canal Street
where he sold radios
next door
to a guy who also sold radios
& how
in the middle of the price war
the guy next door
said to my grandfather

      Moe, what're we killin' ourselves for
      come
      let's be partners
      we'll knock down the wall between
          us

& he told me
how he had started his own bubblegum
      company
shortly after he got out
of radios
only to sell that off too

& then he stopped

he said he hadn't talked to his brother
in over 50years
yet they both had retired to Florida
& lived only a few miles apart

how one night
he sat in his car
outside his brother's house
& watched through an open window
as his brother drank coffee
& watched tv
while my grandfather thought about
growing up
on the lower east side
& a $2000 loan
he never got

he never got out of the car
either

       couldn't, he said
       didn't know how

◆ ◆ ◆

I threw the pictures onto a shelf
turned the etch-a-sketch
upside down

gave it a good shake
righted it
& began
  slowly
methodically
to expose
how far I've let myself run
only to return
for the 2nd & 3rd time
until I threw it all
back
into the carton, folded
over the flaps
& shoved the whole damned thing
under the shelf
& just sat there
absently resting my hand
where my finger found its way
to a glass shard
broken off from a framed portrait
I didn't remember

I searched that face
for something that would tell me
why he never let me know
his family

why at this funeral
we didn't know who to notify
or how

why neither my grandmother
nor my mother
wanted his ashes

why he & I stopped talking

& as I walked downstairs
carrying his image
back to the office
where he had spent so many years
& gathered so much dust
I noticed
I had begun to bleed

Absolution

As we drove down from the north
on route 1
I could see the tired skybreak
of a Boston where I'd lived
years before the changed faces
had disguised
the old haunts
& quiet backalleys
I walked on slow summer nights

& I could still hear my footsteps echo
off the old rattling windows
on the hill still

see the streets glisten
under gaslamp glow
the summer after I moved
back to Boston
& a 4story tenement
I'd never seen

      & I could still hear the neighbors
      across the alley
      (it's the heat
      as the humidity
      stifles their words
      she
            drops
      a bagful of garbage
      from the window opposite
      so he pounds
                down the stairs
      as he pounds out his rage
      scoops up their garbage
      as she leans out
      to demand his attention
      but he is already back upstairs
                with the garbage
      she throws down again
          he goes down again
      & all I could hear were their angry tones
      which sound
      so much like my own

I have to leave

out to the old haunts
& quiet backalleys
I walked on slow summer nights

We pulled into town
& after crossing the hill
drove down
past a school that discarded
a 19yearold addict

    & I could see myself
    tripping down Huntington
    on so many wasted summerschool nights
    past the Museum
    past Brigham Circle
    looking for the right
    left turn
        up Tremont
    & out to Delle Ave:

I call Dave
& we drop on the phone
        (& again later
        & again later after that
stuff
a few packs of cigarettes
into the pockets

of my pinstripe overalls
maybe grab a beer
             or 2
& head off
to lose a game of strategy
because I had none of my own

so frustrated
I throw the pieces
across the room
& we crawl calling
for the lost   little blue piece
                 little blue piece
until we collapse in a pile
of drugged laughter

his cigarettes long gone
we each light one of mine
the matchtrail lingering
as I blow the smoke
at the distorted reflection
in the mirror
which hangs
on an otherwise barren wall

& when the smoke steals my face
I wait to see
if I've been wiped clean
by the last curling wisp

or if the face returned
is no longer mine
but it is
so I try again
& again
& again
    .

When we drove the first pass
down Tremont
& I didn't see the
turn
saw instead
                    the changes
            & under
    that the old
            familiar drugged
                    up disorder
                            of
    a Roxbury
    ruin

I knew the neighborhood

but not
where I had been
        large buildings still familiar
        so much torn away
        redone

on an unfamiliar road
about to cave in
my heart
with a nervous energy
I'd never named before
in that blown
southbronx landscape
of a Boston
I hadn't seen
in 15 years

We'd gone too far
up Tremont
when something called me back
the other way:
        a sign
to take another U
turn
    & a right up Parker
    to the next block:

    Delle Ave

    .

You listened
as I remembered the reason
Drew
    Dave
& Neal

moved
        to the Brookline student ghetto
where I lived
that next winter:

how I came upon
Drew
the day he was robbed
        at knifepoint
in his own apartment

how Dave had found him
bound to a chair
gagged
        & crying

how we helped him forget
in a mist
        of   alcohol
                tobacco
                & drugs
                        until
all we could do
was watch him
under black light
& strobe
        catalog
the meager possessions

left
        by the bandits
        .

I wanted to be strong for you
I wanted to say
        See See
        I survived all that
        & boy was I cool
but I couldn't do it
while you sat next to me
in the car
silently
watching my face change

as we turned up Delle Ave
& you looked for #7

I saw you peer
in some dim entry alcove
the front of the building
newly bricked
        a car backing toward us
        along the narrow 1way street
        its rear window
        broken out
        passed
        on the sidewalk
& I remembered

the pale faded green
of the old clapboard face
as we drove
through
the neighborhood
                    turned
down a sidestreet
blocked

& still wasn't sure
what had happened
so long ago
that I ran so hard
        & so far
numb
to the days & the years

I wanted to believe
in a single childhood event
so terrible
it set me off
& I knew
I couldn't pin it down
because a chronic condition
was no longer
        a moment
I could deny

& then we were downtown
as mystically
as 4 guys
with about $3.50 between them
who bought 2 gallons of gas
for a VW bus
that ran on 3 cylinders
& used the rest of the loot
for a bottle of Mad Dog

I told you
how it made me crazy sick
at Jamaica Pond
while Ted skipped rocks
Monte skipped out
& Dave slept it off

how it all made me crazy sick
all those nights
.

We parked the car
& were walking
past the commons
where I wanted to tell you
100 other stories
& couldn't remember
how any of them

were
     fragmented

through Govt Ctr
to Faneuil Hall
a mass of people
everywhere
I looked: a place
         I drank
everywhere   I drank
a place I forgot

distracted

by the misdirected memories
I couldn't make whole
       & which lapsed
into a confusion of incomplete
nights
     waking
on those summer streets
not knowing where I was
when I was
     so broken
      .

You watched me
out of control
        slipping

back into the cold

so we ducked
into a place for lunch
                  & they were rude
& we ducked
into another place for lunch
                  & they were ugly
so we ducked
into another place for lunch
                  & they ignored us
& you said
take me to the car
I want
to get you
        out of this
it hurts too much
to be here
.

At the car
you were hungry
having not eaten
so we went back to the inn
at Sturbridge
             for dinner
ordered too much
& brought it with us
as we drove down from the north

to New Jersey
            & I assembled
the broken bits of stories
I couldn't hold onto in Boston
& talked
just plain sick
for 4 1/2 hours
until we were home
& I had nothing
left
.

You drew me a bath
to soak you said
to soothe

& as I slipped
through
the steamy wisps
into water
& saw the absence
of my image
in the fogged mirror
the heat
        unbound
every muscle
relaxed
        & I was five

I webbed my fingers
with soap bubbles
& remembered
what happens to a child
when a momentary
need
for attention
is filled
with a busy vacuum

when
the time it takes
isn't taken
by a mother whose
cold eyes
       knit
with the image
of a father
whose depressed face
sleeps
before the endless tv

when
the only place to hide
is the nowhere
at the end of a long ladder
extended
from a toy fire engine

and I begin to understand
why

on the way out
we passed a man
selling
          raffles
the money goes to a 1/2way house
for recovering addicts he said

as I clutched the ticket
deep into my coat pocket
& held it there

we talked
about my first return
to that place that had beaten me
when I hadn't any strategy
and he told me
about his brother
dead
          of his addiction

& as I rose
from the cooled water
with a 5yearold boy
who had cried peace with himself
I smiled at the presence of my image
in the cleared mirror

Robert Cohen

remembered
the terms of surrender
& slid out the other side
clean

.

The Wait

i start up the computer
and wait
i open a piece of software
and wait
i sit at the keyboard
and wait

i wonder:
how many poems
are lost
in this abyss
of useless time

i am always on line
for something—
                    waiting

it starts in the 1st grade

a teacher says
take out your notebook
and a pencil
and some kid named frank
with premature acne
and dirt under his fingernails
from helping his father
rebuild the engine
of a model a ford
all weekend
can't find his pencil

okay, the teacher says,
frank can't find his pencil,
let's all wait for frank
(who wants to crawl
into the darkness of forever
never to be seen again,

it's all of us
each wishing we could just
give him a pencil
or just
make the teacher
go away

or maybe it's 3rd grade
the teacher
fumbling at her desk
for her lesson plan
while william
the kid who sits in front of me
plays some kind of linear billiards
with the counting beads
strung across the front
of his desk
until mrs rothstein distracts herself
by scolding him
for holding up the lesson

when was it exactly
that i learned how to wait
learned how to sit
in a kind of endless limbo
and do nothing
while wandering the long
dilapidated structures
of an overstuffed mind

but since i seem to have time
to waste
i saunter past recollections
of old blackandwhite reruns
on afterschool afternoons
and miserable sickday
morningshows clearly awful
the firsttimearound

i'd spend the day in bed
taking medicine, sleeping
or drifting in daydreams until
i'd snap to and stare
into the flickering
in a state of alertness
ready for whatever came next

it's brooklyn
half a lifetime ago
when i could stare out the
plate glass livingroom window
to anna & izzie's house
across the street
and while i wait
for their daughter's name to
flash across my consciousness

i remember the family with
the 2 girls, carrie and donna
who'd lived there before

and then something
a flicker
a flash
a change in color
the light shifts
against my retina
i am drawn to the screen
the machine is waiting
for me to begin
this poem

Faith

I stood on line
in a chinese takeout place
on 9th ave
while the owner
leaned
his back against the counter
& spoke
on the telephone

I wanted to know
how
an american phone
could speak chinese

as if the technology
were languagedependent

& I thought
of all the prejudice
I was taught
about foreigners

    that each country
    has a separate history

    that all those people
    in all those places
    are different

    that this
    is america
    & our technology
    is ours

do you picture china
with phones?

    or do you see
    a peasant
    farmer
    in a coolie hat
    & loose garment
    in a paddy

hungry
or perhaps
at work
       bent over
some old piece of equipment
in an antiquated sweatshop
in a rickety seaport warehouse
where there are no downtowns

this man
who spoke chinese
became more
& more animated
until I realized
his voice
was translated
by a device
which does not remember
conversation
yet carries out
an ordered transfer
of energies:
       his voice
broken into parts
disassembled
& reassembled
in a demonstration
of 3rdgradescience
where atoms
are made of parts

so small
that the distance between them
is comparably vast
as in a solar system
where most of everything
is made of nothing

is this the logos?

No. it is just
cheap talk

    & I wondered
    who
    was on the other end
    of the line—
    a chinese man
    in china?

        do you see him
        in a 3pc suit
        briefcase in hand
        as he stands
        in a tall building

        an
            important man
        with a corner office
        one window
        a view

                    of the waterfront
                    the other
                    of the countryside
No.
he spoke to a different china

                    —the one downtown
                    is a selfsufficient village

                    a bunch of brownstones
                    where gardeners work underground
                    old apothecaries
                    have potions for everything
                    & the gangof4
                    wears leather jackets
                    knives & chains
                    a west side story
                    in chinese

& because the words that carried
across connections
were messages
of a confused culture

chinatown
in a broken down universe
tells us
how it is

each mystery
lessens the number of things
we understand
about democratic laws
that lets a chinese man
speak his ancestor's tongue
on an american phone

    laws which last
    & work
    only
    as we believe in them

did we want phones?

Doctrine tells us
to stay on the line

    just hold on
    it will work better
    once we find the explanation
    for all of this
    we can harness

    this universe, understand
    its every machination
    an autism
    which barely initiates
    its own language

it keeps
every last bit moving
when we already know
what it means to believe
that the way we have come
is not
the way things are

THE
KRANTZMAN
STORIES

Krantzman Plays Pong
Mid-'70s

HUSHED WHISPERS, MUMBLETONES swim, Jeff hands across another Heineken and the Pong pings its electronic buzz. And Murray Krantzman wins one and is there again, ready to play again, pours his earlier winnings into an empty mug—the one the bartender rescues and Krantzman's going *NO not that leopard piss* . . .

It's dark in the *Cask and Flagon*; there's not a lot to see amid the beeryreek of cheap wooden tables and spotlit lengthened bar behind: the rousing noise of the collegecrowd guzzling pitchers and pitchers and pitchers: roll the camera left and right and all you see are shadows. The jukebox blare drowns all but the most shrill voices, it's not late, just dark, and it's fall, early fall in New England when the colors of the day inspire the druginduced colors of the night and the black and white screen of the Pong machine mesmerizes again the regular crowd, it's newness as novelty, and left there is Krantzman, back to the crowd, elbows tablebound, sortofcontrolled fingers controlling, numbnosed beer mask squeezing his vision blurred, but not yet, not quite: the electronic ball approaches his paddle, shortened now by the compensatingcomputer to give his opponent a chance, up atop the machine the opened warming Heineken won so far, Krantzman waiting for his roommate, waiting for his date: wishing he knew why he agreed other than that promise to a friend.

She's an easy one if she ever shows, everybody back home used to get some from Lynda and there he was biding time waiting his turn at the Pong machine, the gray noise seeping in the periphery and the ball passes his paddle and BEEP, the point, lost, his opponent gets the serve, score is 9-3 Krantzman but he's losing focus, losing himself inthebeer inthecrowd inthemusic inthedream: okay, tighten up, pay attention.

"You're deadmeat now: watchiss."

And Krantzman slams the serve back with strong english, a wristtwist to the circular controller, a digital bounce to the lower corner accelerates then a digital bounce up and across only to slow again with contact at the upper border, his adversary returns it freely, easily and Krantzman again spins the controller and the ball bips wildly this time up to the opposite wall, where it slows on contact, drifts lazily down across to the bottom of the screen, opponent side, midway, contact, bip, and takes off like lightening for the center for the opponents barrier and opponent, not suspecting the spin, arrives too late and BEEP.

10-3 Krantzman.

He no longer has a body, just this Pong machine and beer to keep him going: was it late? Where was Jeff, where was Lynda, how do you get out when you don't know where you're in? And the serve belongs again to Mr. K who rips off a power slam straight across the centercourt to his opponent's unaware but lucky paddle and straight back again to Krantzman who leaves his paddle and the volley is automatic, rigid, as he reaches up again to the top of the machine, drinks down his guzzleofbeer, turns back to the game at hand and spinning english to the lower corner defeats again a worthy, sober-er adversary: to the victor another Heineken.

"Whose quarter's next?"

"'Zats Maxiz."

"Well, get 'em. Siz turn."

Swivels back again to scan the door, a tall thin shadow topped with unruly wiry hair: it's Jeff, the roommate beckoned and returned: Jeff to the rescue, to the retrieve:

"Hey man, take my winners, you can have somma da beer. Mus' be six or seven up here."

"You got it: seen Tennen?"

"Nope."

"Keep your eyes out, he's got my money."

"You got it."

And still no Lynda.

Krantzman
Remembers Orson and Ward
Mid-'70s

ORSON ON THE RICKETY BACK porch of Ward's apartment. Orson wearing this squirrelly denim hat with the brim turned up, his little round glasses and quirky smile that always made Krantzman think he knew something Krantzman couldn't, as if the dark secret designed to always make the dream turn sour was his and his alone. And there was Ward gangling next to Orson, absently knotting and unknotting a length of rope in his long bony fingers.

The three stared into an empty summer sunset behind an old Roxbury tenement disturbed (the three of them, not the tenement) only by the sound of an anonymous trumpeter pleading with his instrument.

Krantzman rose to peer out over the railing, noticed a bat slowly circled overhead. Wondered where it came from. And why.

"Don't lean on that," Orson warned.

Krantzman drew a wrinkled pack of cigarettes from his shirt pocket. "Got matches?"

"Inside."

Krantzman walked into the darkened apartment, switched on the light, scattering the roach hoedown dancing in the center of the kitchen floor. Krantzman tapped the last cigarette from the pack, tossed the empty on a pile of garbage near the sink, and glanced around until he located matches on the gray Formica table near the porch door. Picked them up. Bent a match backward and scraped it against the striking ribbon without tearing the match out of the book. Lifted it faceward. The flame roared in his ears as he drew the familiar hot smoke down into his lungs where it soothed his jangling nerves. Tossed the book back on the table, the spent went bent upwards. Step one.

Step two was in the refrigerator on the second shelf: cold beer. He found some eggs in there as well, and some butter. Food was a treat—when had he eaten last?—and the only trick was to find a pan clean enough to cook in. Outside, Ward's ears pricked up at the sound of Krantzman simultaneously cracking open a beer and clanging and banging through the cabinets, clean-pan searching. Ward sauntered in, seated himself in the only available chair, drew the ashtray to within comfortable reach, and resting his elbow on the table let the smoke from his already-lit cigarette rise through the stillness as he watched Krantzman, manic as ever, oblivious to Ward yet somehow aware of him smoking and chuckling softly, gather himself to cook two scrambled eggs.

Krantzman threw a dollop of butter into the mostly clean pan he had located and placed on the stove, wiped the knife's remaining sheen of yellow onto the edge of the pan, then set it (the knife) down, and turned on the gas as high as it would go, a bright blue flame erupting over the edge of the pan, singeing the edge of butter as he turned back to the counter to prepare his eggs. By the time he had found the pepper, the melted butter had begun to burn. Krantzman bolted to the smoking pan and gave the butter a swirl with the knife's tip, carefully draining his beer in the process. As he whirled the pan, the remaining but still relatively large lump of butter in the pan's center was sent flying across the room, landing with a sizzle directly in front of Ward.

While Ward wiped away the butter, Krantzman set down his empty beer can, placed the pan back on the flame, went to the refrigerator, and stared at its contents. The liquid remaining in the pan began again to blacken and smoke, the charred smell hovering above the pan. Krantzman leaped back to the stove, turned down the flame, broke the eggs into the pan, attacked them with the knife to break the yolks and create a semblance of scramble, then turned and closed the refrigerator door.

Krantzman was thirsty.

He scanned the counter near the stove, then the counter near the sink, then finally the table. Only empties, including the one he had just finished. He went back to the refrigerator and absently drew a can from the second shelf, popped the tab (which he tossed on the counter), drained half of it, found a fork to replace the knife he'd been awkwardly using, and finished scrambling the almost-cooked eggs. Ward lit another cigarette as he settled back into his chair, watching.

Krantzman reached into the outer pocket of his overalls, pulled out an unopened pack of cigarettes, tamped them filter-end down and, carefully choosing the correct side, opened the pack. He wrapped the red tear string around the oblong piece of wrapper to which it was attached, pinching the middle into a butterfly shape, placed this in the ashtray before opening the foil and withdrawing the first cigarette from the new pack. He turned to the stove to light his cigarette, slid the pan to the side, lowered his face sideways to the burner, took a long somber drag, placed the pan back on the flame, and turned to Ward who pointed at the stove behind Krantzman, gesturing gently toward the evergraying eggs. Krantzman, having made a mess of his food, turned off the flame, brought fork and pan to the table and ate, blowing on each bite to cool it off, and offering alternate mouthfuls to his companion, who politely refused.

Krantzman had been drunk for several days and the hallucinogens he had taken a few hours earlier were beginning to confuse his perceptions even more: he liked taking the drugs because they allowed him to keep drinking almost indefinitely and that was something he enjoyed as much as the psychotic episodes where he watched himself drunk—he called them out-of-body experiences, slow-motion movies projected onto his brain, and it didn't much matter who else could see the movie or whether he was functional at all: he was having fun, and his friends had fun watching.

With hardly enough booze in him to counteract the burgeoning effects of the acid, Krantzman wandered down the hall, turned into the bathroom, shut the door, and adjusted himself in the mirror. Within seconds he had not only forgotten what he had gone there for but had also noticed that there was something different about the bathtub; it had no drain. How did the water get out? Krantzman made a mental note to ask Ward, realized he had better get back to his friend because he (Krantzman) had been gone for what seemed like a very long time, then washed his hands. As he looked around for a towel, he noticed that not only had the drain in the bathtub returned—a cue to the true nature of his hallucinations—but that now the door to the bathroom had itself disappeared and been replaced by a smooth and unblemished wall, perfectly white, perfectly perfect. No cause for alarm, at least not yet. Instead, Krantzman got undressed, took a shit—a mildly spiritual experience in and of itself—got dressed again, and went back out to the kitchen to finish his eggs without troubling to notice that the door had gone and replaced itself.

Alone in the kitchen (he assumed, since he didn't see Ward, but that again could have just been the drugs),

Krantzman searched for the rest of his eggs. He had gotten used to filling in the blanks, making decisions about his own behavior based on external evidence, and the pan was not where he had left it on the table, only a large brown ring as if someone had once put there a very hot something and burned the Formica.

The pan was in the sink and empty; he must have finished, or Ward had changed his mind and decided he (Ward) was hungry after all. Krantzman dashed past the fridge, stopped, wheeled, grabbed another beer—having at some point between bathroom and kitchen finished the second half of the one just recently opened, and realizing now that only one more six remained—and skittered down the long hallway past the open bathroom door to Ward's room at the far end.

The room was more shooting gallery than bedroom: a single table with a too-bright lamp, an old dresser, and a bare mattress on a bare floor. Krantzman sat in his usual spot near the door. Ward (who was here after all, and not in the kitchen) passed the pipe to Krantzman and as he (Krantzman) took a long easy hit, all the edges came off the world, he (Krantzman) was comfortable within himself, the walls slipped into place. This was a safe house.

Somewhere in that room his mind went blank: Krantzman took another hit and his brain was a dancing darkness of faded sound: music he didn't dream; his body.

◆ ◆ ◆

And it was time to go.

He grabbed his beer, put on his shoes, and began the trek up the avenue and back to his own apartment, his own bed. There were lost hours, time spent walking and walking and walking, always a slow and steady plodding eastward to the new dawn, the new sun. Krantzman needed to continue. He came to himself amid the trees and water in the Boston Common, a place to rest while he waited like a lizard for the sun to warm him.

He sat near the pond, smoked, and dozed. The colorless predawn dispersed moments of nodding sleep, cigarette would burn down, burn his fingers, startle him to stub his smoke in the grass, to light another. Others around him doing the same, each leaning against a tree or sprawling on the grass, each locked in his own hideous silence: and there was Krantzman chilled by the dewy wetness seeping through his clothes, tired, wired.

He rose, thrust hands into pockets, turned his back on the sun coloring his world, and drifted back across the park, back across the silent escape from his fear, past the crazyman come once more to lecture insanity at the Great Elm, back down through the searing gray eyes and jaundiced memories marking time.

Krantzman Meets Lynda
Late '70s

AND THERE WAS KRANTZMAN again, standing at the Brooklyn bar again, weaving on his feet again, feeling the oppression of others around him, the loud music blaring unintelligibly past his drunk ears, the white bip of the Pong machine flitting in the corner of one eye, the old black magician cadging beers from rich white college kids, all too interested in themselves.

Krantzman had gotten too drunk too fast; he wasn't able to follow much or see very far beyond his immediate awareness of the well-lit bar itself: there were spots recessed into the ceiling overhead and the lights shone directly down the long wooden bar, backlighting almost everything else. The place was a cave, a dark half-flight of steps down from the street, never too crowded save on weekends. It was a trading post and a meeting place and a conference room, a rallying point from which to begin a night's adventure, or a safe harbor in which to end one.

For Krantzman it was usually a beginning. As the backlighting allowed everything to fade and fade further, the laughter became derisive and distant—Krantzman, selfconscious, there to meet Lynda, a set-up made by an old friend from the old neighborhood who hadn't been part of Krantzman's life for years, and she would be there soon. Hopefully. This time.

He wanted to slow it down. Krantzman turned to the bar to order another and as he reached for his almost-empty mug, reached out as if for help, there to take his hand was the old black magician who shook it vigorously up and down, dragging him back into the bar's aura, back to drunk again, out of control again, dizzy and discordant one more time, words slipping, eyes slipping, just this one more time: survive. Then the black man dropped his hand boisterously roistering the crowd of nonlookers and onlookers aloof, the black man who reeked of musty clothes frayed at the edges, unshaven, unkempt, clothes worn and worn out, shiny, a threadbare collar on a yellowed white shirt, the tie long lost. The magician took Krantzman's hand again, led him out of his silence, and thrust into his anxious palm something . . . soft and dry and very compressible. He wrapped Krantzman's fist closed around the object, closed tightly and Krantzman knew the magician was fake, he himself an unwitting shill for some old bartrick hustle but the crowd moved in closer and there were faces darting in and out of light, attentive faces listening as the magician spoke the narrative of fakiry; the story makes the trick worthwhile.

Was there money on the bar? Krantzman didn't care to remember and the black magician's narrative must have seemed funny because they all laughed—no more nonlookers now, only onlookers—and he knew they were laughing at the story he couldn't remember hearing, the magician's gray foam cubes on the bar, three of them sitting in a row, saw the black man press them into the hand of a girl who had also had too much to drink, giddily smiling now laughing her innocence as this black man touches, her face changes, she controls herself and responds to the joy of the moment, the laughter a little weaker, a little thinner. Krantzman all the time staring vacantly hearing and not hearing, wobbling from foot to foot from front to back as he tries to maintain his composure, leaning on the bar, the laughter crescendos again, the loud music drowns him again, his grandmother's fragrance drifts out of thick cigarette smoke and crowd surrounded by a flaming red mane: it is Lynda, and she is there looking for him, and he is there at the center, an unwitting and unknowing celebrity, turns to introduce himself, the song in the loudspeakers fades, the laughter rises to compensate for the emptiness, the voices hum and buzz everywhere, the magician pulls Krantzman's hand forward over the bar into the light mumbling an incantation prying open his hand and three gray cubes are revealed to the stunned crowd, the girl forgotten, her hands emptied by the magician's sly underthetable removal of evidence, and Lynda turning to the action, stumbles and falls into Krantzman, jolting, jostling his balance his one free hand wrapping around her body to hold her up and regain his balance at the same time, he, jostled, into the bar stands upright, releases Lynda.

◆ ◆ ◆

Lynda.

◆ ◆ ◆

Krantzman has been living with her for six months, almost since they'd met. Promises made.

◆ ◆ ◆

And it has been two months since her brother Clyde had moved in under the guise of an extended visit.

◆ ◆ ◆

Last night he wanted Clyde out, the angry demand interrupted by Lynda's mother barging in, using a key Krantzman didn't know she had, wouldn't have wanted her to have, Lynda's mother setting down her two suitcases, announcing she had left her second husband, that she too had come to live with him (Krantzman) and Lynda. The second husband appearing in the open doorway moments later to claim both prize and luggage, the brief exchange between the two, Lynda turning and running to the bedroom at the end of the hall slamming the door behind her as Clyde emerges from the bathroom opposite waving a plunger claiming *I fixed it! I fixed it!* Clyde's mother taking in her son's shitstained clothes and idiotic expression, turning to her spouse, shrugging and walking out the door, husband and luggage in tow. Krantzman collapsing on the couch opposite the vacant doorway staring into the empty hall. How much more?

Instead of sleeping he wandered the neighborhood streets, out along the junction, always a few bars active even at two in the morning, casual hookers on parade along the avenue, street gangs looking to rob innocents who didn't know enough to make themselves unappealing, the always-open news stand always selling pornography and journalism. And cigarettes.

The decision to drink (again) came easily. He had forgotten his promise to Lynda. Marty the bartender who hadn't seen him lately set him up and Krantzman's friends watching TV at the end of the bar and Marty the bartender wanting to know *what's the story how come you ain't been around* and all the talk about how he thought he was in love. And as he kept drinking he stopped calling Lynda by her name, she became *bitch* and his speech slurred; he was talking to Marty his old friend; at closing time he's out on the street, too late, too guilty to go home, the cabs still waiting in the junction, the hookers gone to houses, apartments, hotels, along the street behind, the entrance to the college, the gate long locked since evening, a sidestreet gate that wasn't closed properly; Krantzman slithered through the space barely fitting through, walked to the patch of grass between the older buildings, sat on a bench at the far end to stare at the clocktower and learn again how to cry.

Krantzman had a job and money and Lynda. There was furniture, heat in the winter, and he was comfortable. He ate regularly. There were new clothes in the closet with his name on them. And then she's telling him how he didn't need the drugs, how she didn't like him when he was high so he just drank, but then she wanted him to stop that too, just wanted him to be different, to be like someone else he didn't know, and her brother Clyde who didn't like Chicago while he was there but stayed for six years came to Brooklyn to complain, couldn't hold a job long enough to get paid and wouldn't have gotten paid enough to move out, except her mother would leave no place for them to be alone anyway: no place for him, for Krantzman, for any version of him.

There had been hope. Lynda had cared for him and that had been enough until he tossed it back, numb to get out of his pain, the white noise coming up through the bourbon, a place to hide behind his anger like a drug he couldn't stop taking, the hours vanishing into themselves with the subtle motion of imperceptible clockhands in diminishing darkness.

Krantzman on Jury Duty
Mid -'80s

MURRAY KRANTZMAN STANDS in the dank postdawn Brooklyn subway station clutching his folded newspaper and listening along the track for the tick of an oncoming train. On a too-early morning that began without sound, the awareness of dreams undone has faded into detail, the alarm of repetition and ritual lost amid the white noise of young go-getters and office strivers and school goers, echoing above a homeless drunk asleep in his own silent stench, the area around him vacant, a demilitarized zone of stained tile. Across the tracks, in comic relief, a fat blonde with over-large features wearing too much makeup, all the wrong clothes, and reeking of cheap perfume catches Krantzman's eye and smiles an emasculating yet lascivious smile.

Krantzman's stomach growls as he denies the grotesque fantasy, forces himself to look away, studies instead the chewing gum at the edge of the platform, each wad ageless yet archaeologically distinct. His eyes follow the scuffed warningline to the slow trickle of liquid which drips onto the third rail, follow back along the stream to the puddle beneath the tipped bottle barely caressed by the derelict propped against the grimy tile wall. He has seen this face before, seen the matted hair, the dirty beard, the filthy clothes and ruined shoes of the shadows, seen it standing in another post-dawn light lecturing insanity to the Great Elm of the Common back from Krantzman's only barely remembered Boston days, seen the glaze descend on the searing gray eyes and jaundiced flesh of forgotten reflections in that garden's pond as he peels back the gauze which wraps the self-inflicted nightwounds' still fresh and oozing memories.

Krantzman boards the finally arriving train, slides mechanically into the seat at the end of the bench next to the door, leans his head back against the graffitied poster behind him, unrecognizable (the poster) and exhausted (him): stretches, yawns. Eyes closed, he arranges his knapsack and newspaper on his lap. More comfortable. Makes himself smaller, less obtrusive.

The train crowds up. Krantzman opens his eyes to survey the car: faces, nameless bodies sit strewn on benches, some standing, leaning on doorjambs, diligent reading of the morning daily, pages expertly folded into personal columns, wistful starings into empty spaces.

The doors snap open opposite. Krantzman quickly closes his eyes against the fat blonde, tenses, presses himself into his seat, his right arm into the stainless steel rail at the end of the bench as she sits near him, the doors on one side then the other rolling shut and the train clacks into motion, gathering speed in the narrow tunnel. The roar of displaced air creeps into Krantzman's consciousness, obliterating everything in its path, drowning the sounds and images of memory in the whitehot pitch of oblivion, his almost sleeping brain lost in an empty reverie and the rhythmic sway of the car. Her perfume again, familiar: whose?

He tried to place it and all he could think of was the black magician, a local drunk who performed cheap tricks for the kids who drank at that bar back in Boston, and the beery reek of stained wooden tables and pitchers and mugs and young drunken students celebrating the everpresent celebration of life's newfound freedoms: first time away from home, away from the supervision of family and friends, the nervous tensions of new friends eager to impress without overstepping bounds—a tapdance of politeness gradually diminished as friendship grows new peer pressures never fully resolved.

"Newkirk!" comes the station announcement.

As the train jolts again and Krantzman is tossed against the seatback, his head smacks against the wall behind and the fat blonde next to him, reeking what he now recalls as a childhood's grandmother-sweet memory-scent of Lynda.

"Franklin! Franklin Avenue! Easter Parkway next!"

Krantzman is suddenly alert, aware of shifting rhythms clacking in the stale air, a train full of faceless people pressing in as he pries his arm from between body and benchrail, rubs the dull throbbing at the back of his head, the crowd thick with the soap smells of freshly laved workers, drycleaning, newspaper ink, the familiar morning odors of an obliviously industrious humanity. No empty straps; no empty seats. Each pole surrounded, held in place by spoking arms attached to a confusion of bags and bodies, closed cases on dirty floors clutched between anonymous legs, all the doors covered, barely noticeable.

Wheels screech, changing momentum as the train turns, the crowd leans, some supported only by the press of others, and Krantzman's ribs against the benchrail. Six stops and fifteen minutes yet to Borough Hall.

"Grand Army Plaza! Watch the doors please!" On a train and going downtown to the courthouse for the last day of his first week of jury duty.

He had no place else to go. At least it was time off from his job, a release from the unfamiliar daily tedium he had taken on since Lynda.

◆ ◆ ◆

The first day had been full of schoolboy images of justice and honor until Krantzman sat and sat on a bench, silently protesting the NO SMOKING sign across the assembly room, some grayhaired civil servant taking attendance *hand in the form please* each juror to receive twelve dollars a day compensation. Who could live on that?

Hours later in another room with rows of semi-comfortable worn-out cushioned chairs, smoking permitted, him with a knapsack full of books, feet propped up on the radiator near the window at the front of the room reading and smoking and reading and waiting and waiting and waiting to hear his name called, to be on a jury, pausing to watch out the window, watch the traffic on Adams Street ebb and flow in and out of the city until he could go home.

And now he wasn't sure.

His name had been called along with a group of thirty-nine others who were led to a courtroom somewhere upstairs, the dingy wood workplace worn and neglected, twelve of the forty directed to the jury box where he heard lawyers each asking the same questions *how old are you have you an education where do you live who are your parents where do they live what is their education?* and the judge asking the same questions again, the lawyers conferring among themselves. Krantzman disqualified for no apparent reason. They can do that, it turns out and he can't ever know why, internalizing instead just another in a long line of losses and rejections and still having to return, no choices no options, hoping at least for a quicker return this time into the room where smoking's allowed.

"Atlantic Avenue! Change for the Long Island Railroad! Watch the closing doors!"

The myth had broken with that first call and Krantzman hadn't like what he'd learned; had sat and read until his name was called and went upstairs to a larger courtroom, the judge's table of marble, a polished wood, top more like what he expected, had seen in movies or on television. Krantzman sitting in the jury box, the judge seemingly wanting to put the criminal away for a good long time, *if you're squeamish about guns leave now*, the girl on Krantzman's right spoke up when asked about her education, the judge too young to be a judge, the defendant a black man fiftyish looking sad not scared as if innocent until proven guilty, the judge talking multiple offenses his comments prejudicial, the jury listening, the fourth group of forty in two days, the lawyers looking frustrated and bored. Krantzman's turn in the hot seat answering and not answering, excused, those who won't cooperate can go downstairs and half the group got up, only the war veteran picked first sat for his chance to put the nigger away.

"Nevins! Borough Hall next!"

Krantzman sets the timing to get across to the doors opposite, pushing through the packed subwaycar without snagging himself on buttons or bags or jackets or jewelry whether held or on the floor, keeping all his belongings with him, sensitive to the whereabouts of wallet, money, keys. He wants to hide in the scent of the fat blonde wearing Lynda's perfume she wouldn't be so bad a place to lose himself in the fleshy folds literally enfolded he wants to hide from Lynda from Clyde from himself his life is taking him back to the street to Orson and Ward sleeping in the park or frying eggs and smoking cigarettes and he doesn't like it because he can feel it this time: the sun coming late enough to catch a train to go to the courthouse early, to sleep to think where would he go he had no one he had no place: Lynda so good Clyde and her family he had no family before there was no place for him to go except downtown his head hurt and the lack of sleep hurt and the lack of home hurt and what could he do but just keep going because there wasn't anywhere else and he needed to rest so desperately and couldn't rest couldn't rest in the chairs in the waiting room where a darkhaired girl came to talk with him yesterday, gave him all those socialist pamphlets she was older would take him, misery the train pulls into the station it's time to go glancing back: the blonde is repulsive stays on the train; he jostles past the last few people who hang by the doors refusing to move to give up the premium real estate the easy onoff and a place to lean, just barely slips through the closing doors onto the platform slings his sack over his shoulder gets his bearings and heads for the stairs.

Krantzman emerges from the IRT into the sunny promenade at Brooklyn Borough Hall woozy, a hangover threatens hurt and throb all day. The clear breeze goes through him, leaves him stunned to be outside in morning light: he squints at traffic moving in all directions, bodies bound from point to point in a pinball game, and for a slow moment the scene has no sound as scurrying bodies sidestep vehicles immersed in a stream of morningrushhour traffic; pedestrians hurry toward law offices, scamper between cars entering courthouse basement parking lots; signal lights pulse green/yellow/red in congealed thoroughfares; forgetful runners hurry off to recurrent futures; restless commuters willing captives in temporary cells.

A sudden lull, the busy scene disappears, the cars momentarily gone, the people inside buildings: an accident stalling traffic up the block. A bus moves into the empty lanes across the street, reveals in its absence a myopic old woman bearing two brown shopping bags, one in each hand, standing in the park.

Lights change. The wreckage of a new car is dragged hanging from the back of a yellow towtruck. Fifty bucks cash for the driver and another fifty for his boss and up through the sidewalk gratings the squealing brakes of another #3 train pulling into Borough Hall Station. The traffic flows strong in front—horns blare, cars zig and zag in and out of lanes, taxis invariably winning whatever race they run; worlds away the old woman sits on the grass, begins to spread her possessions on the ground as another bus pulls in, obscures her again.

Krantzman turns to the concrete concourse lined with fenced-in trees and grass, scattered benches. KEEP OFF. Grass for observation only. He crosses the clamors of irate traffic, turns left again past the liquor store at the far corner and down a half block to the Chock full o' Nuts.

The cafeteria buzzes. Krantzman can't follow the chaotic conversations around him, standing still is dizzy, the line too slow, the acrid aroma of fresh coffee mingles with the sweet morning smell of breakfast cakes, sticks in his throat, everyone neat smiles, ready—

"Regular coffee, extra sugar."

—yawns at the lady behind the counter electric blue houndstooth moves too quickly trains abruptly return as quickly—

"Thirty-five cents."

—hands a picture of Washington to the cashier, takes the bag on the counter, his change.

"NEXT!" her shrillness startles out to the cool March morning.

End of the week: he can't imagine they'll call him today, resigns himself to boredom, reading, conversation with people met. Krantzman turns right into the rude blast of a trucker's air horn, leaps back to the sidewalk while carefully protecting the bag holding his too-hot coffee, speedwalks to the revolving door of the New York State Supreme Court building, the same faces every morning in the lobby, stops, takes a deep breath, gathers himself to the empty day through the wood door ASSEMBLY ROOM past the church pew benches sparsely populated by prospective jurors each with book or newspaper, walks down the left side of the room, already registered he steps past the office past the screens that didn't hide the freight elevator, the ladies, the water fountain, the mens. All neat again the wood arm chairs. Into the smoking room; two men smoking cigars a woman engrossed in the *Daily News*, early enough to get his seat at the far left in front near the big glass windows, the radiators to put his feet up, Adams Street, the little park.

Krantzman slides his knapsack off his shoulder to the floor, drops his newspaper on top of it and sits. He

takes his coffee from the bag, dumps the sugar packets, stirrer, and napkins in his lap, places the coffee
and empty bag on the chair to his left, removes the lid
from his cup and places it into the empty bag. Shakes
down the sugar and tears, pictures of birds. He dumps
the four packets into the cup and stirs gently, sips, the
coffee's had time to cool just enough, puts the cup back
on the chair, takes out his *Times* to begin the reading he
couldn't on the train.

Krantzman still thick with the booze in his blood,
the lack of sleep, is unable to concentrate, tosses the
newspaper on the dormant radiator. He is tired, very
tired. He takes a sip of coffee, cigarette would be just
the thing. Setting the folded *Times* on the windowsill,
he checks his shirt pocket finds a wrinkled pack and a
new book of matches, extracts the one bent cigarette
left, straightens it between his fingers stroking the
length of it several times until he can smell the tobacco.
He places the cigarette between his lips, strikes a match,
watches until the flame engulfs the treated head, brings
the lit match to the cigarette and inhales. No draw. The
butt is broken, the paper wrapper torn.

Krantzman tosses the cigarette and match into the
ashtray at his right, reaches for the knapsack on the floor
at his side and as he continues to lean over, the dizziness
becomes acute and he just grabs his sack onto his lap,
stops to breathe: that was work. He reaches to his left
for his coffee, sips, replaces the cup. Unfastening the clo-
sure to his knapsack with his eyes closed he folds back
the green canvas cover and rummages past the books and

papers all folded among themselves to the separate compartment in the inside front, pulls out a fresh but slightly flattened pack of cigarettes and another book of matches. Nothing worse than not having matches. Except not having cigarettes. He checks. There is still one more unopened pack in the compartment.

With eyes open, his vision blurred. Krantzman taps the new pack filter-end down and carefully chooses the correct side, opens it. He wraps the red tear string around the oblong piece of wrapper to which it is attached, places this in the ashtray before opening the foil, tapping the pack gently against the closed side of the top so that a couple of cigarettes slide forward an inch or so, withdraws the first cigarette from the new pack.

The ritual dispensed with, he strikes another match and lights the cigarette: the lightheadedness from the lack of oxygen is just enough to offset the burgeoning hangover. The numbness fading as the alcohol fades, Krantzman places the knapsack back on the floor next to him and sets himself in his seat. His coffee in his left hand, his cigarette in his right, feet up on the radiator he can watch the morning movie and relax. After this smoke, another shot at the paper.

No pressure. Comfortable and absolutely still, the pain in his head subsides. Did he have aspirin in his sack? Always used to have a bottle. Look soon.

Krantzman takes a long hard drag off the cigarette and holds the smoke deep in his lungs for an extra second, blows out toward the partially opened window in a measured breath, creates a small cloud momentarily opaque.

He stills, not breathing as the cloud clears.

Krantzman takes a sip of coffee, replaces the cup on the chair, looks at his cigarette burning between his fingers, watches the glow of red embers at the end, follows the abstract patterns in the smoke until the red has turned to gray ash, he flicks at the ashtray but it falls to the floor, takes another long somber drag to relax, holds it, and watches as the smoke propelled out of his mouth in a controlled stream strikes at the window, this time curling in under itself, shattering the window's light into thousands of shards suspended glistening in silence, the smoke drifting out and over the window sash, out and above the traffic; Krantzman watches in amusement as it circles and dances in deeper and deeper patterns until the window the street the room completely disappear.

◆ ◆ ◆

"Your attention please, jurors. Please report back to the assembly room for afternoon duty at 1:15. That's 1:15, jurors. 1:15."

Scraping chairs rearranging, prospective jurors standing, talking, sitting and standing again, newspapers folding, the rattling sounds of people moving through the assembly room.

"Al you got 26, Nick your down eight, Barb's got four, and I'm in trouble. Whose deal?"

Disembodied voices all around Krantzman slumped in his chair, sits upright abruptly to cough again, clears his throat, opens his eyes to Adams Street, his right hand still holding the filter of a burned out cigarette, the length of ash shattered on the floor.

He glances at the cold cup of coffee on the chair next to him as the sun's brightness glints off a passing chrome bumper, searing his eyes, his hangover. Hungry. Time to eat.

"Don't do that, man. Take his knight."

Krantzman gathers himself to stand, flicks the filter to the ashtray, grabs the strap to his knapsack with his right hand pulling it to his shoulder, stuffs both *Newsday* and *Times* into the sack with his left, haphazardly folded, turns, stands to face the room empty save for the chessgame, a few scattered readers, a man shuffling a deck of cards while reviewing marks on a scorepad, his lips moving silently, adding subtracting adding. The blood rushes up to Krantzman's head, knees weaken, he grabs a chair, the strap sliding down weights his arm, eyes closed to gray and heaving rapid breathing, stills. Almost. A morning gone.

Krantzman and a
Squirrel Dine al Fresco
Mid-'80s

SUNSPARKLE BRIGHTBLINDING glares through wide glass doors, Krantzman squints a cigarette to his mouth and holds it unlit between dry lips, pulls his coat tight against the too-coolness of the spring day. He fishes for matches in his breast pocket, finds none, leans his shoulder to the clear brilliance of a revolving door and wheels reeling out to street and sound: a crowd herding to lunch, lowing across sidewalks as he blinks the chrome off parked cars, a moving cocoon of light constricts around his head the dullpressed throb of nonsleep, not enough sleep, and the need for more. Not that much time for lunch, but he'll take it: anything beats the waiting waiting of the almostjury room.

Pants pocket. Front right, front left—no matches. Can't remember where he put them. Rear pockets empty, he kneels among the streaming hungry to ransack his sack for fire: cigarettes, books, papers, pens, yes. His hand withdraws and slips open the rubbed worn cover of an unused pack, white tips of old matches dried, crumble. Krantzman rips and strikes flame, draws the match to the cigarette still dangling and inhales as the eddying air behind passersby blows the match dead. Legs all legs, suits and pants, shoes and heels clackwalk beside him. Again: select, strike, and the head of the match flies off into space. Dead match toss and again, now two together, strikes and cups hands, moves to and draws the flare of fiery matchheads, the cigarette burns, he takes a long slow drag, stands, the draw of cigarette from dried lips stings, tugs away skin stuck to filter tip, the smoke expands.

Krantzman coughs and spits as he replaces the matchbook in his breast pocket and pulls his knapsack crosswise in front of his body, bumping several as they pass, *oops sorry 'scuse me sorry*, his voice muffled by a passing containertruck belching thick blueblack smoke as it rumbles the sidewalk. He takes another quick hit and flicks the full lit butt between bodies to the curb, the hazy backdrop dissolves the silent moment when the driver shifts gears and drones away. The muffled voices of lost conversation restored, Krantzman turns up the street to follow salesmen and lawyers, judges and politicians, all: the patterned rhythms of midday downtown traffic doomed to repeat itself tomorrow.

Woozy boozy Krantzman dances briefly with a gust of arctic air, a cold blast unexpected even on this cool a spring day, it bites at his already redfaced face. Lynda's friends would be arriving for the weekend from somewhere this afternoon, a French Canadian girl she knew in high school, what's her . . . Monica, some others Lynda never met. Krantzman shivers against the cold, turns the corner.

The liquor store stands across the street in the middle of the block, its unlit neon sign grayed by citysoot and grime, the streaked plate windows thick with faded ads and old displays calling over the rushed subway passing beneath the grates underfoot. He crosses, enters, purchases a halfpint of JackBlack, places the package safely in the center of his knapsack, and leaves quietly, without incident. Food first, or he knows it won't stay down.

Krantzman crosses back again to the busy swell of lunchcrowd sidewalk, sights a sign for PIZZA—HEROES and heads for the open door. Once inside, he catches the counterman's eye and orders.

"Meatball hero. Extra sauce. Large Coke to go."

"Cheese?"

"Yeah, okay."

"Provolone?"

Krantzman nods, what else would it be? feels the heat of the ovens as they open and close, hears the office girls as they giggle their dripping cheese, turns to see them finger food slipped neatly into mouths redlipped and opened round to swallow, nibble gently the tips of triangle slices, pie folded over, the slippery oil softening the hard crust, drips slowly pooling in the paperplate below, the hot white cheese stretching dangling from the mouths of the young girls, almost liquid as it flows under its own weight, suddenly swallowed. Behind the counter slams of white dough on the hard metal tabletop, silent fingers kneading the expanding dough freshly floured, freshly pounded, roundturned and twirled, tossed and laid gently on a flourbed to be covered and slipped into oven heat.

The register jingles the exchange of coin and paper for food, the patrons move on to tables, the girls, filled and spent, slip easily out while Krantzman watches his sandwich pulled from the oven wrapped and bagged with a can of soda, napkins and a straw.

"Two seventy-five. Anything else?"

The register rings again. Krantzman digs deep to random folds of paper cash and hands across three George Washingtons, waits his change, a different George, round and wrinkle-edged, turns as he drops the coin into his pocket, walks out the door. On the street he shifts the knapsack's weight from shoulder to shoulder switching the bag of food from hand to hand as absently as he moves toward the court building, his mouth salivating, his sour stomach nervous, knotted.

Krantzman turns up the street toward the park.

Quickening his pace with purpose he shoves past the shuffling mass on the sidewalk, steps off the curb and slips between rows of meters and cars to dash through halted traffic to the island median where, wheezing and dizzy, he pauses: inventory and adjust: sack, Jack, sandwich, and smokes: the blood rushes as he tightens his grip on the weight of the sandwich in his left hand, clutches the strap of his knapsack high on his right shoulder, leans forward turns head checks traffic, the rising pulse rate of onrushing vehicles counterpoints the rhythmic throb in Krantzman's skull as he calculates his opening, races the rest of the way to the park entrance, momentarily sprawls across a greenslatted bench, drops the knapsack to his right, his food to his left, and still wheezing gathers himself to the ground where he lays his sack open toward him on its back, the unopened bottle still in its brown bag tucked safely among his books and papers.

Krantzman sees the morning's baglady sitting on the ground, watches her remove her dark glasses, peel her tattered boots from her feet and pick thickcaked blackdirt from her toes as he pulls his wrapped sandwich from the white paper bag, unravels the greasestained paper, stuck cheese, steam swirls, the soursweet smell of overcooked canned tomato sauce and meatballs rising makes his mouth water. He spreads his food before him, the can of Coke in his right hand, tears his hero along the incomplete slice, leaves part to rest on its translucent wrapper, and eats hungrily the other, barely stopping to gulp and breathe, chewing and chomping without ceasing his clattering jaws.

Heyhey you gonna eat allat yself whaddabou me aincha gonna save sommadat fuh me I dint eatchet tday eedah yknow cmoncmon gimme somma de odder half okay i jus stan here an watch okay okay illbe quiet no chitterchatter okay waddya say just a bit a bite okay

The squirrel chittered and chattered and fretted, pacing back and forth between Krantzman and the old lady ignoring that longtime friend and park denizen the bag lady watching Krantzman instead, eyes and head jerking anticipating as Krantzman eats his sandwich greedily.

Nonuts nonuts whassamadda aincha nevva seen a squoyul bfaw mungry ytink its easy t suvive innissity whaddaya tink huh ill telya whaddaya tink cos its like dis dat lady ova deah she don nevva gimme no food an I don fin noplace tget nun mungry man yknow I seen ysit onna floor an righdaway I know ywas one of us cos it aint offennat sumbuddy sits onna floor wid us like dat so like yknow whyt doncha share dat food huhhuh

Krantzman watches as the squirrel paces nervously back and forth eyeing the food. With the last swallow of the first halfsandwich still working its way slowly down his esophagus, Krantzman begins to fidget with the second as the gulps of air trapped below the clot of food shift and slide until the peristaltic motion of his innards press down and a channel is created: air rushes upward, escapes in a loud rasping belch.

Wawassat wawassat hoboyhoboy ygonna make dem kind noises fum dat food I don need nonnuvvit whatsit you eatin anyways huh ainno nuts I ainnevva seen no lumpy nuts bfaw heywaidaminit dats blood don smell like blood sos maybe it aint whatsis ick a woim geddouddaheah fuckin woim ill move ill move okayokay donchoo goway wid dat food um comin back

The squirrel bolts across the grass scurrying right through the old lady's newspaper where he encounters her feet's reek, instantly freezes, dances in a circle before hurrying back to the spot he had just occupied and stands stock still, his eyes locked with Krantzman's.

Unnoticed, the baglady removes her torn topcoat to reveal a faded sweatshirt several sizes too large for her bloated body. Folds her coat carefully and places it across her boots and dark glasses resting on the newspaper to her right while muttering to herself in a low and thickly garbled guttural phlegmfilled voice. She quiets, then lifts her right hand up under her shirt to scratch as she places her left index finger to her left nostril and presses it closed. The baglady turns her head to the right and release a one-shot snot which lands just between her body and her coat. She begins again to mutter.

See dat see dat dat ol lady duzzat alla time don evn know she doin it no maw batso crazy um tellinya batso crazy she bin innis pahk ferevvah and olways binna same jeez duh stawreez I cd tellya y gonna eat dat stuf or wut huh huh

Krantzman looks away, takes a long swallow of soda, replaces the can to his right, eyes the paper bag just jutting from his sack: soon. Reaches forward and grasps the uneaten remainder of his sandwich in both hands to keep the saucemoistened bread from flaccidly falling, pauses; a low snore saws in from somewhere unseen while Krantzman takes in the parksmells of grass and earth, shifts his weight, raises the cooled and congealed sandwich as the squirrel flinches and fusses a few feet away, absurd: how could a squirrel?

Whaddya mean how I cn tellya ennyting abou wut goes on in dis pahk ennyting at all like frinstance see dat sailer ovah deah snoozing he bin heah since las nite abou 2 inna mawnin come heah with dis lady not so much a lady kinda reminds me uh dat bagady back deah de tings she says yknow like she mumbls alla time dis same stuf yknow like shes maybe sum kinda stuck recud er sumpin bout wen she wuz yung an had dis hot date like she wuz wid dis guy fer a coupla drinks inna coupla places anna next ting deys driven see in his cah see an waddaya tink bud dis guy cracks up de cah an shes got no maw dat fud duh nite an she goes tuh dis waterin hole wut she bin hangin out in de kinda place dey got maw den wun bah lotsa tables inna dahk kinda place maybe aint so cleen kinda place wuts got music onna weeknds annay cleah a spot fuh dancing

The kind of place where the familiar reek of beer-piss and booze mingles with the essence of cheap perfumes, the kind of place that's downstairs, below street level, like that cave where he met Lynda, thinking she would be his for the night for that one night only, she leading him by the drink to a dark table in the corner to talk but kissing him hard and leaving almost right away with the promise to return later that night, he turning back to the bar.

An de ol lady goin outside tuh get ridda dat uddah joik she was wit oilleah yknow dat bozo wut couldn drive ennywayz he come lookin fah her telin em how he neely got em kilt an it ain no good times like dat so get de fuk outta hea an him takin ou dis nife like heez gonna mess up her face an she jus runnin

*bak inna bah an sittin atta table inna cawnah husself lookin
scared anna bitthirsty*

Steadying his glass on the bar with both hands,
glancing back to see Lynda returned, knowing he
couldn't stand to be alone after her touch had left him
hopeful, ordering two more drinks and bringing both
to the table slurring, blurring, the lights brightening to
last call and leaving, rising to follow her lead back to
her room.

*Naked an he wuz onner an den she wuz onnim and den
she sez tostop she getsup an goes inna batroom toins onna
showah an sits onna turlit stahts playin wid husself yknow
just tget husself reddy an he getsup to leeve den she comes outta da batroom and fuks em as good as she know how an den
she gets crazy batso crazy like I sez stuffs evvyting she got inta
an old duflebag an jus leevs bin onna streets evah since loined
tuh fuk fuh money and den got wor out jus bummin afta dat
like sheez still looking fuh sumpin yknow hey ya gonna eat dat
shit or wat*

Murray Krantzman, having followed Lynda's lead
from Boston to Brooklyn so she could be near her
family, forcing him to be near his, doing whatever she
asked just to have a warm body to lie with at night,
following instructions just to be loved. He places the
barely eaten halfsandwich back in its paperwrapper,
reaches over to his knapsack, pulls out the brown bag
JackBlack, removes the bottle and stares at the label,
not seeing the words at all.

The squirrel rears up on his hind legs sniffing the
changing air, his front paws prayerful as Krantzman,

unscrewing the top, cracks the plastic seal, tips the bottle to his mouth and knocks back several hard swallows. He rights and recaps the glass flask, places it back in his sack.

Rushing flushed and hardbreathed, Krantzman drains his remaining soda, tosses the uneaten half-sandwich to the squirrel, crumples the can and the sandwich wrapper, places them inside the unflattened empty bag, checks again that his Jack is safe, and reaches to his breast pocket for his cigarettes. He withdraws the pack, notices the unopenened matchbook tucked safely inside the cellophane wrapper, laughs softly to himself and reaches back into his breast pocket to find the other book of dried-out matches, tosses it aside, shakes his head. Krantzman taps a cigarette from the pack, cups it in his left hand and lights it, replaces the diminished pack, lifts his knapsack to his shoulder, and rises to scan for a litter basket.

Across, the baglady leans left to her shoppingbag, withdraws an old green armyblanket and spreads it unevenly across her lap. Krantzman watches as she begins inspecting the frayed edges until, suddenly standing, she drapes the blanket across her torso, arranging and rearranging the fabric until it holds to her satisfaction on her misshapen frame. Then, bending to rummage in the bag to her right, still mumbling, she scatters several pairs of sunglasses on the ground along with other detritus before settling on a pair of mirrored aviators and a flashlight which she raps on the ground several times. Then, reaching her newspaper to her chest with her left hand and holding the flashlight up over her head in her right, she stands erect, her features momentarily frozen as she marches liberty-like and barefoot out the far end of the park to the cadence of her own voice.

Krantzman
Mostly Listens to Testimony
Mid -'80s

LUNCH OVER, HALF FOOD AND half food and half booze, Krantzman turns toward Adams Street, striding purposefully back toward the courthouse. Pausing at the curb for traffic, Krantzman puts a cigarette to his lips, exhales a thick gray plume and freezes, numb and empty. Wind tumbles across the Brooklyn Bridge, funnels and accelerates down Adams Street to blow his ashes away, dissipate the smoke, fan the bright red ember glowing brighter beneath the shadow of a passing cloud, faded light soothes his burning bloodshot eyes, a hot fragment of tobacco sweeps up and whirls against his flesh, his hand, stings, startles, he looks down at the quickburning cigarette pressed between his fingers, raises it back to his lips and drags deep once more off the smoking butt, exhales, flicks his thumb against the filter tip, and careful to look both ways tosses the cigarette into the carrying wind, crosses to the shadowed and opaqued revolving doors.

Inside, the echoing tick of heels on marble marks time, the grayfaced clock above reads thirteen minutes past: no time, knots his stomach tighter, the blood rushes up, dizzy as he plunges through the open wooden doors, ASSEMBLY ROOM, tighter, down past the portrait of George up front, left, faster, to the smoking room where the stalesick stench of tobacco reeks tighter, quickening, closer around his throat, in staccato breaths, ducks behind the worn screens, a swinging door MENS no apostrophe: the sewersweet urinestink invades his eyes, nose, the green door stall slams open and he is wracked in a single convulsion to purge; now dripping and emptied his nose burns, the taste is enough to press on his knees the knots tighten *please*, his stomach convulses again, purges again, now the liquid, the clots of food, the brown liquor he can taste it all, see it all as it burns out through his mouth and nose, pools in the porcelain beneath his face, crying, *no more PLEASE NO MORE, never again*, reaches to his left for paper to wipe his slack face, his body, clothes unscathed, knapsack dampened on the sweating floor with bottle safe. He cleans around the bowl and flushes, wads the paper up wipes his face and snots long and deep spits again clears his throat, flushes again, stands still dizzy, the dull echo of the stall door slams his rattled hurt as he hulks over to the sink, runs the cold water to rinse his face takes a mouthful: rinses spits repeats.

Krantzman reaches with his right hand to the paper towel dispenser. Holds his body up with his left, grabs a wad of coarse white paper, wets and applies a makeshift compress to the back of his neck, then cups his hand under the running stream of cold water and rinses his face, his mouth again, spits staring at the draining whirlpool swirling too fast, his breathing normal as he leans now on both hands, sleep, Lynda, looks at the old mirror and before his warped image the PA cracks to life: *the following jurors please report to room four, that's room four, jurors: Archibald Harris, Ronald Dixon, Susan Smith, Elnora Nescire, Joseph B. Donnetz, Murray Krantzman, Annette Scarpa ...*

Me.

Motherfucker.

Krantzman straightens as he shuts the water, gathers himself as best he can, tasting the breath he needs to cover, cigarette, no time, a shot: Jack's better than puke, reaches down into the damp sack and removes the half-pint that always seems to be there, carefully protected, unscrews the cap and downs a long series of swallows, burns through him, shivers, warms: better, stable, steady-hands, returns the cap, stuffs the bottle back into his knapsack, tucks his shirt in quickly, lifts strap to shoulder and walks weakened warily out the swinging door.

In the hall the attendant, blue uniform, third-world infantry, the Internal Director of InterOffice Traffic, ushering, bellowing: *room four jurors, room four ...*

Another officer at the front of the small windowless room, blank walls, two tables behind him, rows and columns of evenly spaced wooden chairs: NO SMOKING, watching the moo-crowd move slowly, speaks:

"I'm going to call the roll. Will the first six names I call please take the first six seats. This is seat number one, seat number two, seat number three, and so on."

Krantzman sits, drops his knapsack at his feet, hears the clunk of the glass flask as it hits the floor, thick glass protected only by the worn green canvas of the sack it rests in, bends forward to lean his head on his knitted fingers, elbows on his knees.

". . . Nescire seat number four, Joseph Donnetz seat number five, Murray Krantzman seat number six. The rest of you can sit anywhere. Annette Scarpatti, Diane . . ."

A tall redhaired woman immaculate in a green tailored suit followed by two slovenly men silently file through the door to Empaneling Room Number Four. The woman sits between the two men at the righthand table near the front of the room: each places a small stack of papers and folders on the table before them. The man on the right, bushy eyebrows, rumpled suit too big, disheveled, nervous manner picks up a pad and fans through the pages over and over, nods to the other man then rises, still holding his pad.

Chairs scrape to muttering movements, a commotion of rustling; Krantzman raises himself up with some effort, stumbles, trudges to chairnumbersix, sits, the bourbon still leveling, coloring, his anger rising, no calls now, musical chairs, the endless redundancy: the blue uniform with the gold badge finishes calling the roll, recalls an old highschool movie: working in the atten-

dance office, going and not going, tearing up his own re-
cords, the mornings spent avoiding his family, leaving for
school, sneaking back to the house to sleep downstairs,
waking to his parents gone to work and him off for the
day with nowhere, no place to go, leaving late, taking the
subway downtown, wandering this same neighborhood,
day after day after day, standing in the same appliance
store watching the same shows, the game shows: solve
the rebus, exes and ohs, guess the secret word.

Snapped back by this room's emcee: "Good afternoon jurors and welcome to civil court. My name is Mr.
Lerner, this is Mr. Osten, and this is my assistant Mrs.
Legatti. Today I'll be representing the plaintiff, Kathy
Feurstein, a former dancer and student from Brooklyn,
New York, and Mr. Osten will be representing the defendant, Barry Goodman. Barry is a transplant from the
west coast, currently a delicatessen counterman residing
on the Lower East Side. Kathy claims that while crossing through the intersection of East 27th Street and Avenue Z at approximately 2:30PM on the afternoon of
August 15, 1983, she was struck by the defendant's car,
thereby sustaining several injuries and inducing a premature end to her dancing career. As with all civil cases
tried in the state of New York, this case will take place
in two parts: first we'll ask the jury to determine whether Barry Goodman is at fault and, if in fact he is, then
we'll ask this same jury to assess damages. But before we
can begin, there are just a few questions."

The same questions, stupid prying questions, as
Wednesday when that day's fatfaced lawyer leaned into

the jurybox: *how many children, how long have you, are you, did you, can you, will you* the woman sitting next to him failing to see the relevancy, the fatfaced lawyer's bifocals slipping down his liquidy nose, wheeling back to his table, to the defendant staring blankly out across the courtroom, the judge rising to admonish the woman, the DA reading furiously at his table, that day's judge thundering at the remaining jurors *this is a criminal case* (unlike today's), the defendant a multiple offender who has appeared in this court before, anyone too squeamish to deal with guns, anyone who cannot divorce himself from his emotions, anyone who cannot judge this case only by the evidence submitted in this courtroom can return to the assembly room now, the whole group save the one man already selected for the jury walking out.

And today: "Everything okay with you so far, Mr. Osten?"

"Fine with me."

"Okay then. Question number one is for everyone in the room. Is there anyone here who is familiar with the defendant, the plaintiff, the intersection, or the accident itself?"

Unclear why knowledge of the intersection should be relevant. Or lack of knowledge. Hands stay down.

"No one? Very good. On to question number two. Question number two reads, 'Is there anyone here who has ever served on a jury before?'"

"I have."

"Could you stand up and tell us who you are?"

"My name is Frank Eisner."

"And what do you do for a living, Mr. Eisner?"

"I'm a plumber."

"Well, Mr. Eisner, I'm afraid we're going to have to ask you a few more questions . . ."

After which the empaneling procedure continues, drones on, finds Krantzman selected to serve and he is not looking his very best and the courtroom dismisses until Monday morning.

◆ ◆ ◆

Opening remarks were led by Mr. L.

He intended to prove that what had happened to Kathy's right leg was worth a small fortune.

He intended to prove that she had had a series of operations and now walked funny and had to remain inactive for the rest of her life.

He intended to prove that she had spent many months going from doctor to doctor and that she had severe damage.

He intended to prove that she had spent much time in wheelchairs and hospitals (perhaps even in one while in the other) and that it had really fucked her up.

First came the testimony from Mrs. Feurstein, Kathy's mom: she told how Kathy was active, fairly popular, a member of her high school gymnastics team, with lots of friends, she could do flips jumps leaps twirls . . . and since the accident was a lump of shit in a cow pasture. She told how Kathy went from one doctor who thought her ankle was broken (Coney Island Hospital's emergency room), to another (not at Coney Island Hospital's emergency room) who did surgery, but that didn't help, to another (still not at Coney Island Hospital's emergency room, or any other part of Coney Island Hospital) who wanted to do another surgery, but then instead recommended her to another Dr., Dr. Graham, a Scotsman who finally fixed her up by doing another surgery, this time putting a metal plate in her leg to keep her bones together and that meant she couldn't even go through normal airport security anymore, the metal on her leg preempting her from attempting the metal detectors, and that meant pat downs which as any woman knows is rude and uncomfortable. And here Mr. L showed a difficult-to-read drawing that was an interpretation of the x-ray that was taken showing all the shattered bones, and then another one, this one an equally difficult-to-read drawing that showed the metal plate, or at least a rendering thereof.

All of Mrs. Feurstein's testimony was in a thick Russian-Jewish refugee accent. Kathy might have been raised a little over-protected.

Then came Dr. Graham's confirming testimony regarding her medical history, what the other doctors had said (and what it meant in English), and what he had done, and the results for Kathy, etcetera. There was testimony about the scars that Kathy had had corrected through plastic surgery, too.

Dr. Graham was asked to draw a diagram of the broken bones in Kathy's leg, but couldn't do it on the blackboard, his skills limited to the deft handling of human tissue but not a finger-thick piece of soft, porous, sedimentary white calcite. We weren't sure why we needed it anyway since just such a drawing had already been shown just one testifier ago and likely from a more practiced hand. And in either case, as Dr. Graham pointed out: "There seems to be a paucity of chalk."

Dr. Graham knew his shit and seemed to be the only person in the courtroom worth anything. He also seemed to realize how ridiculous the courtroom was.

The jury was sent from the courtroom several times during the morning when Dr. Graham testified while various legal and moral issues were reviewed, deemed just potentially damaging enough to the cases of either prosecution or defense to allow the jury to hear, and was then called back one time, only then to be dismissed for lunch, something that routinely happened well before noon and stretched, as far as Krantzman thought, for either too short or too long a time.

◆ ◆ ◆

The Honorable Court Justice John H. Molton stood and addressed the court: "Mr. L.," he said, "you may call your next witness."

"We call Kathy Feurstein."

A carefully and well-rehearsed exchange transpired before the eyes of the jurors. Kathy testified to where she was when she got on her bicycle, her path, where she got off to walk it, where she got back on, that the street was crowded, why she went the way she had rather than her usual way, which way she had looked, whether she had glanced up or down, right or left, all in all that she was involved in an accident. She recalled with entirely unbelievable clarity every aspect of everything she did and saw. Even whether the defendant was looking at her or behind him as he reversed out of his parking spot and hit her. She remembered where she fell—only a foot or two from the car—in the crosswalk. And of course, she even remembered details of things that had happened immediately after she was hit. She remembered the condition of the bicycle. The feel of the scraped skin. The glare of the daylight. The heat of the asphalt (and the cracks in it) against her legs. She expertly recalled everything that happened to her four years ago as though she were describing it happening right in front of her. As a witness. Which, in fact, she was. The absurdity of the situation was, of course, that she had to do that in court or her testimony is unsure; but how much detail can you recall about anything that has happened four years ago? Even the things that were done and you think about after? One tends to lose the sharpness of the image, the fragments become distorted and jumbled and some of the clarity lost. But not for Kathy Feurstein.

Time ran out at 3:30 and the jurors were sent home.

◆ ◆ ◆

The remainder of Kathy's testimony came the next morning; then followed the testimony of Benjy. Benjy was a carpenter who had found Kathy's bicycle some twelve or fourteen months later in the police station. He testified to it being mangled when the real description showed it to be just a little bent out of shape. Adjectives.

The plaintiff's attorney rests. Then a short break. Hard to move but, sluggishly stretching, manage to get to the hallway. Walking up and down, shoes squeaking on the overpolished tile, the sound irritating. Head not much clearer than yesterday. Out too late. Lynda. Sip of water from the fountain. Need and want the backpackJack, but MENS no apostrophe room experiencing expected breaktimetraffic. No time, no place.

Returned and seated. Judge arrives fifteen minutes later. Privilege. Says finally to the defendant's lawyer: "Call your first witness."

"I call Barry Goodman."

About time. Almost fell asleep. Definitions of justice don't work as well as good coffee. Both lawyers out to prove the facts in this case lead to only one rational decision. What was it he said about? . . . oh . . . no mention of injuries or damages. Only have to decide fault. Keeps the question of money out of range. That's another court session. Down the road. Another jury too? Or the same one? Me again?

From the back of the room came the hulking Barry Goodman wearing suit too tight and shirt too small, said shirt having its lower button open, permitting one large roly-poly belly to protrude just slightly, enough to draw the eye. Distracting. The slob was sworn in.

"Now Mr. Goodman," began Mr. O., "could you tell the court exactly what it was you were doing at the time of the accident."

"I was drivin' m'car."

What kind of question is that? What else could he have been doing? Three years to check to see if they have the right person? Can't be.

"What kind of car would that be, Mr. Goodman?"

"A '67 Dodge Dart."

"And what color was the car?"

"Green."

This chair isn't comfortable. Plastic seats make me sweat. Sticky and hot. Still want something to drink too. Can't have anything. Only judges and lawyers can. Even then only water. Sit here on the shelf like a toy at the disposal of a child's caprice. How did I let myself? Could be downstairs with the others, reading. Learn things that way. Not subjected to endless intolerable nonsense. Who cares what color his car was or whether he honked his horn? Guy's a slob. Can't speak grammatical English. Mr. O. either.

The judge doesn't look like he's paying attention. Writing in that damn book. Can't believe this is real. Should just go home. Can't of course. Civic duty. Rule of law.

What now? A blackboard again. Chalk diagram of the intersection. Guess they found some somewhere. The scene of the accident. Wait a second. I know where that is. I didn't realize. That street's not far from Nostrand Avenue. With that little park there. Maybe inverted? North points down. Wonder why they? Never saw one like that.

"I see. And tell the court, if you will, Mr. Goodman, was East 27th a one-way street where you were parked or was it a two-way street?"

"One-way."

Where he was parked, maybe. But it's one-way on one side and two-way on the other. Wonder if that has any bearing. She could have come up the wrong way on her bicycle. See later.

Wish I had a bicycle. Did once. Frame cracked. No wonder either. Down that ramp near the highway and into a ditch. How I didn't crack, too, I don't know.

"Mr. Goodman, could you tell the court, according to the diagram, which direction you were heading at the time of the accident?"

"I can't see."

"You may go over to the blackboard," the judge directed. Barry Goodman lifted his weight and plodded to the blackboard. Peered.

"I was goin' this way." Pointed.

"Could you please state what direction that might be?"

Mr. Goodman studied the diagram carefully, intently, finger oscillating. A puzzled look grew on his face. On every directional diagram he had ever seen, north pointed up and west pointed to the left. However, on this particular diagram, for a reason as yet unknown to any in attendance on this occasion, north pointed down and west pointed right. The same imbalance this situation lent to the courtroom was tremendous; Mr. Goodman was, indeed, lost.

"I was goin' . . . west. No . . . east." Finger steady.

"Mr. Goodman, in which direction were you headed?"

"East." Finger moving.

"Are you sure of that, Mr. Goodman?"

"Yeah. East." Finger steady.

All right, Mr. Goodman, would you take the chalk and draw a line showing the path you took pulling out from where your car was parked, until you stopped."

Mr. Goodman picked up the piece of chalk and again studied the diagram. Slowly, cautiously, he drew a gently curving line depicting his path. He started his line (according to the diagram) from the southern side of eastbound East 27th to the eastern side of Avenue Z headed north. E 27th Street, however, runs one way north to south and there is no parking on the side of the street from which he began this mystical journey. In effect, Mr. Goodman had started from the wrong side of the street and moved forward, turning the wrong way down a one-way street. His confusion was obvious. Chalk and finger now moving, unsure.

"Your honor, if I may assist my client," pleaded Mr. O., "I can correct his error."

Error. It's not his fault he's so stupid. Court's helping him, though. Diagram is upside down and backward. Ingenious tactic: whoever dreamed it up? Why do they do that? For purposes of clarity? To avoid confusion? Real masterminds.

Mr. O. strode to his client's assistance and together they corrected his path.

"May I proceed, your honor?"

"Go ahead."

Mr. O. double-checked the statements that Mr. G. had made and asked the same question several different ways when he felt Mr. G. was getting himself in trouble. Mr. G., bright star that he was, didn't pick up on it at all.

◆ ◆ ◆

Then came the closing arguments.

Mr. L. had pressed all the witnesses as hard as he could, and reaffirmed their testimony in hopes of a huge payday, a third of which would then be destined for his own bank account. Mr. O. played the stereotypically defeated hero, sullen and giving ground at every turn, seemingly resigned to failure and reduced to cheap tricks. He begged the court and jury for leniency and asked that, if they did find against Mr. Goodman, that they wouldn't damage the family's financial well-being too much, though he never really said what he meant.

◆ ◆ ◆

Then came the deliberations.

During deliberations, after being treated to a passable yet sober lunch, the jury was making cracks about holding out for dinner. Krantzman didn't participate in the jollity, nor the banter.

Discussion: Krantzman drew a diagram of the intersection for the architect, then the architect, from the exuberance in his voice, was able to explain clearly the distance represented. And all considered it, took a vote, and found unanimously in favor of the plaintiff.

Before giving our "we have reached a decision" statement, everyone reveled in their work, complimented each other on a job well done, relaxing, some with cigarettes and pipes, and laughing and making cracks about the different people involved in the case, themselves included. The architect was pronounced foreman by design, since he occupied seat number one and therefore had to give the decision to the court. He hoped no one would get mad at him, said by him in jest.

◆ ◆ ◆

"Has the jury reached a verdict?"

"We have, your honor." Pause. For effect. "We find on behalf of the plaintiff."

Mr. O. stood. "I wish to remark that this outcome is contrary to fact, contrary to law . . ."

A scare ran through the entire jury. Nobody heard a word past this, yet all calmed themselves and realized that the man, like all of them, was only doing his job.

Krantzman and the Stray
Mid-'80s

KRANTZMAN CLEARS, RISES the subway's flight of stairs to the street, straightforward eyes cresting the top step to big furry paws: a dog, a wolfish, reddish, brownish, pointy-snouted dog sitting on the sidewalk just behind the blue streetframe which surrounds the stairway exit: he is a big dog with a fox face and sharp, triangled ears, wagging and smiling, waiting, watching each passenger rise and pass along to the sidewalk and away; not mangy but disheveled, unkempt looking—as if it had spent the afternoon loping through some underbrush, not hunting exactly, but curious and perhaps puzzled by random odors—and when Krantzman rises into view, the dog throws his head back, snout straight up to the sky and wails a howling, shivering, trailing sound that at once causes all heads to turn and Krantzman to smile.

"Hey boy, you looking for someone?"

The dog stops and drops his head to look at Krantzman, his (the dog's) tongue hanging from the side of his mouth, panting, not drooling, in the cool of late afternoon. The sun is low in the sky, the moon rising just opposite, long shadows cast from buildings, and the dog staring straight into Krantzman's eyes as he (Krantzman) stands above the animal, looming. Krantzman takes a long hard drag off his cigarette, flicks the barely started butt to burn down along the bus stop curb, and exhales slowly the soothing plume of bluegray smoke, upward, into the sky, then kneels to the dog, careful not to let the backpack slip, and reaches out to pet him.

"You lost?"

The dog raises his front left paw and knocks Krantzman's hand away, then closes his mouth and nuzzles his snout under Krantzman's arm. *No, I'm not lost. I'm waiting. For you.* Krantzman bends closer and the dog licks Krantzman's face as he (Krantzman) scratches the thick fur behind the dog's ears and along both sides of his neck, wonders what kind of breed he (the dog) is, or how mixed up.

"Well, I've got places to go. You want to come with me? C'mon. Let's go see Marty."

Standing, adjusting the shoulder strap of his bag and watching for the dog, they proceed forward through the busy sidewalk steppers and around the corner to a quieter avenue, the edge of a different neighborhood.

Marty's wasn't very far off the junction, about half a block up on the right just past the shoe repair shop. A heavy wooden door by a darkened plate glass window, a small red neon sign at its center that says " ART 'S AVERN" in the darkness behind the glass—although the "Y" had been know to flicker on for brief moments after several months' rest. Along the low sill gathering dust were beer signs and logos and a few long-forgotten softball trophies left behind after one pick-up league celebration or another.

"Okay dog, this is the place. Let's go."

With that the dog again looks right up into the sky, throwing his head back to let out that long atonal howl yet again, the few passersby turning to see what's making the sound then turning as quickly away as Krantzman opens the solid oak door to the dimlight beeryreek of an old neighborhood gin mill. The dog pushes past Krantzman to the center of the room and freezes, his nose carefully sifting through the scents, seeking the familiar, marking out the dangerous, and finding his path. Slowly the dog looks once around the room then walks right up to the bar and jumps his front paws onto it as if an old hand ordering his regular. Krantzman closes the heavy wooden door to Marty's mocking voice addressing the dog.

"Hey. Hey. HEY! What is this? You can't get served in here." Then turning to Krantzman: "This guy yours?"

Marty's behind the bar with a fistful of empty mugs looking from the dog to Krantzman and back again as the dog opens his mouth to pant and impatiently bats the bar with his right front paw a few times. *Yeah, I'm thirsty, too. Get me something.* Then the bartender puts the glasses down and rubs the dog's head, scratches behind his ears.

"I'll bet you're a thirsty dog. Let me get you a bowl of water. C'mon around the bar. C'mere."

Krantzman turns to the bar as the dog jumps down and walks around to the end and disappears behind, softpadded feet noiseless on the old tiles.

"I don't know if he's mine," Krantzman says. "I found him when I got out of the subway just now. Or maybe he found me. Like he was waiting for me. So we came here. Do me a favor: never mind the dog. I need a drink."

"Just hold your horses," Marty says. "This guy's thirsty." Marty takes a bowl from a stack at the end of the bar, one of the ones used to feed peanuts to the bar-stool-sitting thirsty to keep them thirsty, fills a bowl with tepid water from the spout above the rinse sink, and sets it on the floor. The dog walks over and begins lapping it up, satisfied both by the water and, apparently, being served before Krantzman.

Krantzman sidles up to the bar and straddles the last stool at the far left end, his old spot near the sink, near the lemon/lime/orange wedges, the maraschino cherries and various condiments, just below the TV, where he can watch the room while he watches the screen. Tosses his bag down on the stool next to him and scans the room, dimly lit as any neighborhood bar, empty booths with low-slung lamps casting yellowed shadows, a few high-tops with stools arrayed around. And the long bar. Aside from an old white-haired street drunk asleep on the bench by the back corner booth, and Marty and the dog, there's no one else here.

"Knocking 'em dead, eh Marty?"

"Hey, it's early yet, nobody's even got off work—or didja forget you're the only one around here who ain't working this week?" Marty stands there drying glasses, looking like every bartender cliché in every 40s' film noir. "Boy, it was good to see you last night. Where y'been?"

Marty looks away from the dog and goes over to the liquor shelf, pulls down a bottle of Jack Daniel's, pours a shot into a highball glass and puts the drink down in front of Krantzman, who knocks it back quickly, shudders, puts the glass back on the bar. Marty knows the drill, pours another, puts the bottle back on the shelf but still within easy reach.

"In love," Krantzman says as he shivers off the last of the cobwebs. "But I think I'm better now. I'm beginning to feel like me again."

The dog whimpers behind the bar. *What are you two talking about? I'm getting hungry here.* Krantzman sits up high and peers over the bar at the dog, who looks back up at him. The water dish is empty. Krantzman thinks for a minute, wonders why he's putting words in the dog's head, imagining. Getting to be a habit. First the squirrel, now this. He'll likely—no, definitely—need more Jack.

"Before I tell you the rest of the story, give him some more water, willya?" Krantzman slowly leans forward, elbows up, to look over the bar. "You got any food for him in this place?"

"Dog food? Why would I have dog food? Wait a minute. I might." Marty's voice trails off as he bends to rummage through the cabinets under the liquor shelf and a few seconds later surfaces with two cans of Alpo, smiling an explanation. "Doug used to come in here with a dog. You remember him? Or was that before your time? No, it was after your time. Started coming in when you stopped and then he disappeared about a month ago. Used to keep some food here because he'd have that dog with him all the time. Ain't seen him. Ain't seen the dog. And this guy looks hungry."

I am hungry, you moron. Can't you see the drool? Stop jabberin' and start feedin'. Jeez.

Marty busies himself at the far end of the bar looking for a can opener when a suddenly loud rush of moving water gives Krantzman pause. Then he remembers Marty's antiquated plumbing and how anyone at the bar always knows when someone's done.

"Hey, Marty. Don't take this the wrong way, but I thought we were alone. Who's in the bathroom?"

"Rick."

Krantzman lifts his knapsack up to the bar and unfastens the two clasps holding it closed. Among the dog-eared papers he pulls out an empty crumpled cigarette pack and a used-up matchbook cover. Krantzman tosses both onto the bar. Delving back again he slides out another sheaf of papers, mixed up messages, some yellowed letters written, unsent, received, unread, two pens, and a battered notebook of reminders, observations, telephone numbers without names, and a somewhat flatted, perhaps stale but unopened pack of cigarettes. Sip. Krantzman opens the pack, crumples the cellophane wrapper and tosses it on the bar with the small bit of foil torn from the corner and taps out a cigarette. He leaves the pack on the bar, shoves all his papers back into the sack leaving out only the notebook and one of the pens, reaches into his breast pocket for matches, finds none.

"Ashtray? Ashtray? Matches? Matches?"

Marty has opened both cans and is carrying them down the bar in one palm to where the dog sits by the empty bowl of water, grabs an ashtray and a book of matches which he puts down in front of Krantzman along with the dog food.

"That stuff smells awful."

And you want me to eat it? Are you kidding? I got a sensitive nose, y'know.

Marty bends to pick up the empty water dish, places it on the bar, and begins spooning the glop out of the cans and into the dish.

I ain't touchin' that crap. Yecch.

He places the dish on the floor in front of the dog as Krantzman strikes a match and lights his cigarette. Krantzman holds on and watches the flame burn down to just above his index finger, then flicks the match into the ashtray where it sizzles in the few drops of water remaining from its last rinse. He takes a quick puff on the lit cigarette, rests it on the edge of the ashtray, careful not to let the rolled paper get wet: that would kill it halfway, waste the burn; the dog looks at the bowl of food and then back up at Marty and back down at the bowl of food, hesitates, leans forward as if to try a mouthful but doesn't, then turns and walks to the end of the bar to sniff at the figure finally emerging with a slight stagger from the men's room.

Don'tcha worry. I won't hurt him.

Krantzman stands up to watch the dog let his lower jaw drop as if to let everyone know he has teeth just as the figure calls out:

"Yo, Marty—what the fuck's wrong with you? Why you got a coyote in here?"

"Hey, Rick. Relax. He ain't a coyote, he's a dog. Followed me from the subway."

"Uh huh. And I'm a white gorilla. Thassa a coyote."

"I was petting a coyote?" a surprised Marty calls over his shoulder.

"Yup."

"How do you know it's a coyote?" Krantzman asks.

"Mr. K., Mr. K., Mr. K. I'm disappointed in you. Smart guy like you should know these things. Hey Marty—where's my sammich? I don' see no sammich onna bar. Where's my sammich?"

"Forgot. I'll get it." Marty turns.

Rick raises his hands skyward in mock exasperation while Marty heads to the small kitchen area behind the corner of the bar to make a Swiss cheese and onion sandwich. Krantzman sits back down, adjusts himself on the barstool and reaches for his cigarette, finds it extinguished in the wet ashtray, paper got wet after all, didn't hear the slight sizzle when the lit end met moisture, just enough to knock it out. He drops the dead butt back, picks up the recently-opened pack from the bar, taps out another, puts the pack in his shirt pocket; Rick takes the next stool over; Krantzman grabs the matchbook from the bar, strikes a match, and inhales the deep bluegray smoke, holds, lets it explode from his lungs, tosses the match to the ashtray where it burns itself out.

"Well, first of all, it's got alla right colors. But the big tipoff is that tail."

Marty walks over to where the two others are sitting and puts a plate on the bar in front of Rick, with the dog just behind him. The animal sits down behind the bar, raises his head straight up, and lets out another low mournful howl.

"And I ain't never heard no dog make a noise like that."

The coyote looks over at Marty standing next to him and smiles.

So I'm not a dog. So what? I ain't here to hurt nobody. But I might if you don't take that swill outta here.

"S-s-something to drink?" Marty asks Rick while keeping a close eye on the coyote.

"Uh . . . yeah . . . make it . . . uh . . . I dunno. How 'bout a dark with a little bit of Rose's?"

"How do you drink that stuff?" asks Krantzman.

"You oughta try it. 'S good."

Marty bends to the refrigerator under the bar,

talking to himself about how does a respectable businessman get into these things? Yeahyeahyeah, nodding at the dog or coyote or whatever. I'll empty the dish as soon as I finish taking care of these guys.

Rick peeks under one corner of his sandwich. "Ya didn' put no mustard on here. Again. Gimme some mustard."

Krantzman reaches past the sliced tart fruit wedges on the tray to his left and grabs a small jar of the hot mustard that Rick always uses, hands it across as Rick nods his thanks.

"Now how'm I supposeta put this on my sammich? Wit my thumb? Gimme a knife."

Marty puts the beer, the glass, and the lime juice in front of Rick.

"Gimme the mustard. Gimme a knife," Marty mimics. "Didn't your mother teach you nothing?"

"Yeah. Gimme a fuckin' knife, willya?" Rick shoots back.

"Just wait a minute. The . . . coyote . . . doesn't want that crap in his dish."

"Never mind that," says Krantzman, knocking down the rest of his bourbon. "How is it you know so much about coyotes? Marty, let me try one of those darks, okay?"

Marty picks up the coyote's dish and empties the contents into the garbage, puts the bowl in the sink and fills it with hot water, hands Rick a knife, finishes washing the bowl out and gives the animal fresh water to drink.

Thank you, but I'm still hungry. What else you got in this joint?

Rick stifles a laugh, spreads mustard thickly on one half of his sandwich, drains his glass, pours the rest of his beer into it, measuring out a small portion of lime juice.

"Gimme another. PLEEZE!! Why don'tcha make the poor thing a coupla burgers?"

Marty puts a glass and a fresh bottle in front of Krantzman and another in front of Rick, who pauses to take a bite of his sandwich, chewing loudly, pouring first a bit of lime juice into Krantzman's glass, then beer, swallowing hard. Rick lifts his glass to his companions, pours half its contents down his gullet, smacks his lips. Krantzman takes a quick sip of the mixture, nods his approval, takes a drag off his cigarette, this one stays dry, and watches Marty open the refrigerator and pull out four burgers.

Rick takes another big bite of his sandwich while Krantzman laughs softly to himself and opens his notebook to a clean, blank page. He takes another sip of Rick's potion, takes a last, long drag off his cigarette and stubs the butt out into the ashtray. Turning back to the notebook, he picks up his pen and begins to scribble, the dried-up ink not flowing, the point almost tearing the page. Krantzman throws the pen down in disgust, takes a long drink from his beerglass and just stares at the wall, the wall behind the bar.

George Washington Reveals Himself to Phineas Phipps

HE[1] COULD HEAR THE RIVER lapping at the clotted sand, the shifting of beached canoes sliding against each other, the tick of rivertide against the sides of the boats in somnolent rhythms softened by the fog come tumbling downstream and settling in the riverbed, leaving only the taller trees visible and trunkless and obscuring the world from sense. Walking out of the woods along the

---

[1] In Cohen's original conception, Phineas Phipps, a foot soldier in the Revolutionary War, was designed as a fantasy-based alter ego for Murray Krantzman, a way to tie Krantzman's personal condition to Cohen's views on the overall culture of the United States of America, which he saw as at least partly responsible for many of the societal problems that the Krantzmans of the world face every day. The plan for the novel was to alternate between extended sections, some taking place in reality (the Krantzman sections) and the others taking place in Krantzman's periodic fugue states (the Phipps sections). This story is the only complete Phineas Phipps segment Cohen left us.

riverbank, his boots crackling on the shards of broken glass underfoot, he is cleaner, fresher. And the fog rolling along the riverbank covering first his feet then the ground; he looks upstream at a dense gray cloud coming but not coming, rolling and folding in on itself and back downstream; three young men as they get closer, their long coats rippling as they move in the thick damp air looking hungry and hostile, one of them, the one on the left, wears an animal skin under his coat, the others in something that might be uniforms, one has a tricorn hat, they all have long hair, the one in the middle pulls out his long rifle and says,

"What's your name, boy?"

And without batting an eye he answers,

"Phineas Phipps."

The one in the middle points his musket, says the General would be happy to know they found one (one what?) and directs him downstream.

Next thing he is one of the boys sitting in a circle around an imaginary fire—the order of the day not to light fires even though the fog and dampness have seeped through just about everything and it's cold—a fire would signal the Hessians on the other side.

The element of surprise he suspects needs to count for something: General George Washington's Continental Army, camped this side of the Delaware on the day before the crossing.

Old JG Birdwell comes along and says he's real tired of being so damn cold and wet this *no fires* shit was about the last straw and he don't care if it is the day before battle it's also Christmas Eve and they aren't supposed to be anything other than scared and nervous says he, has him a few jars of good old barley whiskey made right here in the colonies and he would be damned if it wasn't now, the time to be drinking them up as none of them might never get the chance again, war being what it is and all—he's the only one of his friends left and since they were all cold and wet and looking for some entertainment they agreed and he agreed to return with the goods.

Morale is suddenly very high. JG comes back with not one but three jars of the stuff and begins to pass one around the circle when Jackson asks JG if he's ever met or seen General George for real. And JG says he's been in a few skirmishes with the man, something to behold in battle—as smart and as fearless as a general ought to be—stands right up there with his men on the front lines if need be, knows when to retreat as well as when to advance, don't make no show of forcing an already lost cause, yes sir, some general, but, he says, you can keep the man.

And Jackson is all up in arms hollering at him "Waddyamean waddyamean keep the man? After all that praise you don't want him or you don't like him?"

JG just stares around, finally says he's sorry he opened his big yap, never you mind what he just said—the big man's a general and that's all that counts.

JG seems pretty bugged by something—like Jackson provoked him—so it gets kind of quiet around the imaginary fire as the jar goes around a few more times and they're beginning to feel a little better, a little warmer, when JG pipes up again, not loud though, looks sort of like he's seeing something where the fire would have been, something he's trying to describe, and as he's talking they can see it too, but JG doesn't pay no attention to that, he just sits back against a tree, opens another jar of barley whiskey, takes a long hard drink and settles in a little, like he's got a story to tell, and starts talking about this Great General, the one supposed to save 'em all who he's gotten to know pretty much by accident.

"It was about thirty of us that was lookin' to catch up with the General—we'd got separated durin' battle—but there was just no catchin' the man; thing was, we'd stop at farmhouses, and the families there always seemed to speak well of him—a gentleman they'd call him, and a giant, bigger than any man any of 'em had ever seen. But seemed the closer we got to here the more likely a farmer was to be angry with him, though it wasn't all the farmers and it wasn't as if they was to badmouth him: what struck me was the wonder in the eyes of some of the women when I could get them talkin' about General George, what he was like. Like they imagined him with some kinda aura or somethin', somethin' a little strange and special.

"There was this one girl, real pretty one called Nancy—said she was gonna marry this Jimmy when the war was over, said he went off with the General. Well, we stayed at this Nancy's house, her father's house, and after we were all settled in out in the barn and thereabouts—

as I recall it was a clear kinda warm night and most of us slept under the stars. We built this big fire, big blaze—and her father comes runnin' out of the house worried that we were too close to the barn and all, how if the wind changed we'd burn down his barn and kill his livestock, and I couldn't figure what got into the man until I saw the jug hangin' off the crook of his finger. When he saw that I saw, he offered it around—we each took a swig, those of us that wanted, and gave him back the jug, and then he notices that his daughter was there too, alone with thirty men. I guess he was about to say somethin' when she went on to him about that she was tellin' us where we could stay and which wood to use 'cause he didn't want us to use his hickory pile for smokin' the meats now did he and besides, she wanted to give us some letters—she waved 'em in her father's face—to get to her Jimmy who was with General George somewhere. At the mention of the General's name her father kinda straightened up and Nancy damn near went into a swoon. Her eyes changed too but not the same as her father's, more as if the girl was in love and I figured she was thinkin' about this Jimmy we were gonna give the letters to.

"Anyway, Pops went back to the house kinda sudden as if he heard someone call him away but wasn't none of us heard nothin' and we began to settle in. Nancy hunkered down next to the fire and rocked back and forth on her toes all the while lookin' in the fire and I saw the light in her big dark eyes—Jimmy had himself quite a woman. She pulled her skirt close down around her ankles and it looked like she was hardly aware of where she was or what was goin' on.

"There's a certain beauty in catchin' a woman just that way—alone with herself, thinkin' things she'd probably never tell anyone. And then I realized she's probably thinkin' of that Jimmy who'd left her only a few weeks before.

"Over at the house there seemed to be some kinda argument goin' on but I couldn't make out what it was Pops was sayin' or even who it was he might be sayin' it to—Nancy had told us when we first rode up that afternoon and asked this girl bent over a big stump if she was sick and if we could talk with the lady of the house, and she said she was it, that her Mom had died some years ago and that she, Nancy, pretty much ran things now.

"Well Nancy just kinda ignored what was goin' on up at the house and reached out and took a long stick out the fire and held the flame right in front of her face. She was lookin' like she was gonna do somethin' stupid so I went to take the stick from her when I heard her father let out a war whoop that would do an Indian prouder than a brave who just made chief—I didn't know what happened to make him holler so but the noise broke Nancy's reverie, she kind of smiled at somethin' that wasn't there and started to laugh: her father, she said, just remembered where his whiskey stash was.

"Soon enough he was bringin' out another jug to share with the boys and he settled in to join us, keeping a bit of an eye on Nancy, but not too much given that this wasn't the first jug. There was a sparkle in the old man's eyes as he talked of the General: seems he himself was too old and too much the drunk to go with him, George had asked—or told him, more likely—that the old man stay behind and take care of his daughter and whatever else came up—a seventeen-year-old girl can't survive alone, 'specially when her Jimmy was gone off to war. Nancy's look faded—my guess was that the possibility of Jimmy not comin' back hadn't occurred to her and the idea put a hex on the whole affair, so to speak.

"So Pops went on about how General George was just about the kindest bravest most reverent clean honest man he'd ever met and the lights went back on in Nancy's face.

"And then he goes on about how there must have been five thousand men all over his farm with the General, and I figure Pops was just a wee bit stinkin' on the occasion of the General's visit—not that he woulda been any less drunk if the General hadn't shown, that much I knew. With Jimmy out in the fields with all these other men, the General didn't think that Nancy would be safe all alone with her passed-out drunken father up in the house—what with his men all over and he really would like to be accountable for all of 'em, but that, man to man, he knew it just couldn't be that way and besides he was the General and rank did have its privileges so if there was room could he and a few of his officers stay up at the house that night?

Robert Cohen

"Pops said it would be an honor to say that *George Washington Slept Here* and of course the General could, he could even have Pops' own bed, he (Pops) would sleep out on the sitting room floor with the other officers, outside the door of his daughter's room—just in case, like the General said.

"By now the old man's jug had gone around a few times and was pretty near empty, and Nils, who was sittin' next to Pops, leaned over to get the jug and noticed in his loudest voice, 'Damn thing's closed to drained seems to me,' to which Pops said not to worry 'cause there's plenty more where that came from and Nancy—who I'd been watchin' all night—told her father that for once in his life didn't he think he'd had enough, done enough, said enough; if there was to be more drinkin' she said, she wouldn't sit here for all the stars and trees to see grown men degenerate before her eyes—that's what she said: *degenerate*—it's bad enough she's had to watch him all these years make a monkey of himself, how she watched her mother leave—she wasn't dead like she told us—how she watched the farm shrink as he sold off first corners then strips of land to keep himself and his only daughter alive—a tirade if ever there was one.

"Well, with that, Nils stood up and made off toward the house to rummage around and maybe find another jug anyway, and Nancy went back to starin' at the flames until the heat melted her angry look, and I wandered off to take a look at the sky and sort out my thoughts.

"I figured somethin' happened to Nancy. I figured Jimmy had sneaked in the window that night and spent it with her and that explained the tirade as if somethin' in her was different now, and she was just learnin' it for the first time.

"I walked around to the other side of a huge oak out behind the barn where I couldn't see the fire or the house, all I could see was all those stars, and I forgot for a moment that I was a soldier at war.

"Then there was all this hollerin' comin' from the house and as I ran closer to it I could make out Pops' voice rantin' at someone tellin' the lousy bastard not to laugh at him. Don't laugh at him! He'll SHOOT YOUR GODDAMN BALLS OFF IF YOU DON'T STOP LAUGHIN' and then Nancy's voice pleadin'. About ten of us got there at the same time—when Pops saw us all he threw down his guns and begun to cry. He just kept askin' *Why'd you let him do it, girl? Why'd you let him do it?* and I figured my thinkin' to be about right. Nils was just glad to get out in one piece and when we got back to the barn he explained that he was searchin' through the house for another jug and discovered that the closet in one bedroom was also a passage to the other bedroom. And when he realized that where he was and where the General slept was the same place and that all those people was sleepin' outside the door to Nancy's room with this passage completely unguarded, he figured there was at least one other cherry tree General George chopped down, and with that he burst out laughin' which brought the old man, who saw Nils standin' in the closet, and Pops realized he wasn't the only one who figured out what musta happened between his daughter and General George so he was gonna shoot Nils to avoid embarrassment. That's when everybody else showed up.

"Seems like almost everyplace we stayed was pretty much the same story. So like I said, you can keep the man."

◆ ◆ ◆

Everything was wet enough to be cold but dry enough not to drip, and Phineas Phipps was drunk enough not to care. He lay on his back wrapped in a blanket, then propped himself up on his elbows lifted his head peered out between spread tentflaps: darker. Several soldiers wandered back and forth at the edge of the fog, beyond them beached canoes and a river he couldn't see but heard. He closed the flap, rolled over and lifted the flap behind: no one, a low hill covered with tall grass, scattered trees, a way out. First stop a barn, find some animal to curl up near, maybe a horse to steal. He shed his blanket slipped out sprinted to the grass at the bottom of the hill. Spread himself flat on the damp ground listening: no light, the fog thick—rely on instinct.

Phipps crawled up the hill through dense brush on hands and knees, paused: something moving and not moving in the grass—not him. Panic lodged in his throat stopped his breathing. He listened toward the sound: a wet slithering groan of male and female rhythm. Slipped his left arm forward to slide likewise, touched bare flesh and froze.

Perhaps it was only a second, perhaps longer. When the poor girl realized a hand had grasped her slender ankle, she took careful stock of the whereabouts of not only her own two but those of her client the Captain, (she, no innocent, rather a woman of easy virtue in the employ of Mrs. Warren whose house rested peacefully just the other side of the hill, and who quartered General George and his officers at the very same moment as this whore did with Captain _____ what she had done already with a half-dozen other officers) and realized that the hand which grasped her ankle belonged to neither herself nor the man with whom she was so intimately engaged, and so followed a short squeal, causing a tension sufficient to startle Captain _____ who, unapprised of any detected interloper, credited the outburst to the ecstasy of the moment and derived from himself therefrom a false ability regarding his sexual prowess; while the young trollop decided the event naught but a cramp in her instep due to the extreme dampness of the night and therefore resumed herself, which motion gave to the good Captain reasonable cause to place his attentions elsewhere.

Phipps shivered, withdrew his hand quickly, muffled a sneeze, and slipped back down the hill unnoticed. He stood erect, invisible in the fog, began again his trek uphill, his clothes soaked from the wet ground, chilled, his teeth chattering, the fog thinning as he crested the hill a thousand thousand stars on a moonless night he could just make out a roof protruding through the cloud which slept below, and headed for the house immersed in the blot that wisped just beyond the hilltop.

With one hand outstretched like a caneless blind man trying to find his way in the dark obscurity of fog he saw the blacker shape of what could only have been a house and stopped.

Heart pounding and temple thudding, his feet unsure beneath him, drunk and tired, cold and uncomfortable, stumbled and shushed as if they were following the orders of another brain, helpless, no choice but to watch himself.

He slid around the side of the building, felt a windowframe and ducked: no light. Nothing inside and the window unlocked swung it open and climbed into a room to move in the darkness, bumped into furniture, warmth, a sweet scent of must old and burning hung in the dull air, sheepish for none but himself, embarrassed by stupidity: they will come now, all of them—the General, Mrs. Warren, the others.

Silence.

♦ ♦ ♦

A girl's giggle disturbing total darkness and another sound, masculine, Phipps trying to sit and pressed against something soft, sagging: under a bed, the weight shifted above, more room. The giggling gave way to cooing, a deeper, sluggish rhythm, the bed breathing above him, flexing the wood frame to creaking, voices pulsing faster, gasping, rapid locomotion releases, sighs slowly.

All his muscles had tensed, hardened against the dust tickling his nose. A foot over the side, large, then another, strode away from the bed. A heavy metallic sound where the feet had stopped, the deep glow of embers cast across him as he turned his head sideways careful not to hit his head on the bed's bottom above him and cocked slightly forward to see the figure of a large man banking a fire.

General George lumbered to the open window, climbed up on a nearby chair and urinated, the sound of his ample stream splattering on the ground outside as a low moan of disturbed sleep escaped from the bed, the girl's acknowledgment of his missing body, his missing warmth: she stirred slightly as the General stepped down and closed the window, walked back to the bed and watched quietly her sinewy arms in the red glow move gracefully once to his absence, pull the blankets closer, adjust her hips with a snort, and fall softly back to dream.

Phipps had only to hope the General's lust had been satisfied—another round would have forced him to show more than his hand—as the General, sorely tempted to return to bed but of higher purpose, removed himself to the adjoining quarters to dress. Phipps slipped out from under the bed, quietly opened the window, and climbed to the gray haze of a fogbound dawn.

◆ ◆ ◆

Phipps rode point in the General's canoe. Gear stowed, he knelt down on his sack at the front of the boat as the rifleman, then the General, got in behind. The second paddler pushed the canoe into the Delaware, jumped into the rear of the boat. Straddling its center, balancing. Phipps paddled slowly, evenly, little backsplash. Easy enough.

He could hear the other canoes slipping into the water, the voices and splashes of mistakes muffled in the dense fog. How many were crossing? The General stood up, the boat swayed side to side in queasy rhythms, and Phipps was scared, sick at the prospect of death pounding the aftermath of strong liquor, late hours, bad weather, lack of food. He was losing concentration, the wall of vapor at the far shore thickening with their approach as if a cloud had folded in under itself, rolling and rolling, the river rolling to, storm and ice rising pelting streaming, a lightning burst at his ear to rock the canoe enough for him to lose his balance over the side, shattering the river's surface, weighted by wet clothes, flailed and sank, flailed and gasped, submerged, taking in water, coughing water out, choking on his own wrong swallow.

AFTERWORD

To Ireland, in Coach,
on Continental

HOW CAN I BE ON A PLANE headed for Ireland and
served horrible tea? If we avoid complexity, we fail to
embrace diversity, differentiation. There is an absence
of mythology connected to ethics and philosophy:
true culture reigns and we get lousy tea on the way to
a nation of tea drinkers.

And now the lights are still on at 10:30p our time
so people, Continental people, can continue to sell
stuff.

I finally get it: "on a sailing ship" (this plane) "to nowhere" (all planes are the same given that there's no

attempt to imbue the flight with any sense of destination ↦ I could be going to Kansas) "leaving any place"
(the same, the same, the same) "if the summer change to
winter" (by travel, then) "yours is no disgrace" (they are
what they are).

In a seat too small on a flight far too long—lengthened
by the waiting—we are held captive by the endless TV,
a commercial we at least have to hear. And we sit, lights
off (all of them, at last), the air cut to very low, in darkness where it is hard to see, impossible to read. And
wait in malodorous limbo (the engine fumes wafting in
as the cabin temperature mounts).

And now the lights work but the air conditioning
doesn't—the child cannot play her games or her DVD
player, a hostage to the absence of conductors for human
serenity.

And who is the brainiac who keeps all these planes on
the runway burning fuel when pressure has already shot
through the roof and the flight attendant who primped
in the mirror in the bathroom with the door open while
my daughter waited is also the one who wore far too
much perfume for the closed—enclosed—cabin of an
airplane.

And then, at Belfast City Airport, on the way home,
where yesterday I called the FlyBe airline to verify what
I could carry onto the plane and what I had to pack—

and the guy I spoke to said I could take my regular carry-on—which turned out not to be true, so I had to repack everything right there on the floor at the reception desk.

Now I bought this pad because I had wanted to jot something down, but I'll be damned if I can remember what it was, so I just wrote this instead.

Acknowledgments

If Rob was here he would want to acknowledge the following people—all of whom helped him to develop his craft:

His many former students from New Jersey, especially Meriam Raouf, Bob Bailey, and Dan Kraines; the graduate professors at William Paterson University in the English Department, especially Phil Ciofarri and Charlotte Nekola; the graduate professors from Teachers College, especially Ruth Vinz and Cynthia Onore; Jane Gangi and Mary Ellen Levin who read earlier drafts of Rob's writing and responded to his work; Michael Charney, friend, writing collaborator and responder; the many recovering alcoholics who supported Rob in his early sobriety and learned with and from him in the decades of sober living that followed, and

Emily Cohen, daughter who owns his heart.

About the Author

Rob Cohen (1954-2016) was a writer, teacher, and consultant who studied, taught, and wrote fiction and poetry. He is the author of academic articles, poems, and short stories, and a co-author of *Deepening Literacy Learning: Art and Literature Engagements in the K-8 Classroom*. Born in Brooklyn, New York, Rob later moved to New Jersey and is survived by his wife, Mary Ann Reilly, and his daughter, Emily.

Printed in the USA
CPSIA information can be obtained
at www.ICGtesting.com
LVHW091319290124
769705LV00010B/882

9 798985 941340